Hey!

I Can Do This

Your Guide To Getting What You Want

Lou Mulligan

1st WORLD
PUBLISHING

Hey! I Can Do This

Lou Mulligan

© Lou Mulligan 2010

Published by 1stWorld Publishing
P.O. Box 2211, Fairfield, Iowa 52556
tel: 641-209-5000 • fax: 866-440-5234
web: www.1stworldpublishing.com

First Edition

LCCN: 2009932812
SoftCover ISBN: 978-1-4218-9114-9
HardCover ISBN: 978-1-4218-9113-2

All rights reserved. No part of this book may be reproduced or utilized in any form or by any means, electronic or mechanical, including photocopying or recording, or by any information storage and retrieval system, without permission in writing from the author.

This material has been written and published solely for educational purposes. The author and the publisher shall have neither liability or responsibility to any person or entity with respect to any loss, damage or injury caused or alleged to be caused directly or indirectly by the information contained in this book.

The characters and events described in this text are intended to entertain and teach rather than present an exact factual history of real people or events.

To Loretta

Acknowledgments

Special thanks to Wayne Campbell, Andrew Tanenbaum, James Mulligan, Evelyn Perricone, Dennis Mulligan, Ian McElroy, Barbara McNichol, Julia Carslake, Rita Post, Dr. Walter Rosocha, Dr. Bob Guns, and Peggy Grall for taking the time to read through and share their comments on sections of the manuscript. Also thank you to the many clients who worked with me as I developed these concepts, particularly Dr. Andrew and Julie S., Peter G., Lisa P., Otto R., Roger and Suzanne W., Karsten and Debra E. The insights provided by The Strategic Coach® Program's founder and CEO, Dan Sullivan, and coach, Russell Schmidt, were also instrumental in my development of these concepts. Members of my Goal Cultivator Community™, including Brett, Paul, Rob S., Gareth, Neil, and Rob W., have also helped me in clarifying my thoughts. There are also many others, too many to recognize individually. Please accept my heartfelt thanks for all your contributions.

CONTENTS

PART FOUR—ACTIVATING THE PARADIGM

PART FIVE—PULLING IT ALL TOGETHER

Preface

Were you there when the grand visionary goals were handed out? You know—the ones that are bigger than life, that inspire legions of people to fall in line and overcome all odds in pursuit of a dream. I must have been tying my shoelaces because I do not remember that part. What I do remember is my parents instilling a sense of right and wrong, of honesty and fairness in me. I remember being told that if I worked hard at something, I could achieve it. I remember key moments in my life when the vision was greater than the effort. As a very young boy, when asked what I wanted to be when I grew up, the answers were always impressive—a fireman, a policeman, an astronaut (whatever that was), a major league baseball player. But I became distracted. I shifted my focus and moved on to other interests—over and over again. When I think about this now, my experience was typical of most people who let just living get in the way of achieving their dreams. I do not think that I did this on purpose. I think that it just . . . happened.

Does this not make me bad? No, it just means that when I get bored, I am distractable. I think this is a positive trait because it kept me from getting stuck in a rut and doing the same thing over and over and over. As a teenager, it allowed me to stop doing things that seemed of limited value—like becoming proficient in Latin—and move on to more interesting challenges. Looking back, I see that either I became the most stubborn donkey on the planet, or I gave in to common sense and looked for the most efficient solution to problems. Nine times out of ten, the latter was the smarter move. Writing this book is the end product of years of this dilemma—common sense versus stubborn donkey-tude. I hope you will agree that common sense is winning out. (Oh, by the way, you will find a few new words and ideas here—*donkeytude*, for example.)

This book is about goal setting and, more importantly, about goal achieving. What makes me qualified to do this? Personally, I have achieved many goals that others might consider major and I am still working on achieving others. Professionally, I am a Certified Financial Planner®. Every day I meet with my clients and observe their struggles to clarify and achieve their dreams. I have developed a system that anyone can use to keep focused on key goals as he or she works towards achieving them.

The idea for this book began over 30 years ago. I saw an ad for pianos in a popular magazine. The copy captured my imagination: "How old will your child be in five years if he takes piano lessons? How old will he be if he doesn't?" Having practiced piano as a child, I immediately knew the answer. "The child who doesn't take piano lessons would be much younger!" My experience had taught me that practicing piano every day can make five years pass very slowly. (Obviously, I missed the point.)

But something about the advertisement stuck in my mind. When I thought about this ad later, I realized the error in my subjective logic. "Both children would be the same age!" Amazing! You would be the same age whether you did something or not. This was not exactly a scientific breakthrough, but it got me thinking: "Then people should do more of the things that will take them towards the goals they want to achieve." It sounded pretty simple, yet how many people actually do this? How many know what they want and purposefully move towards it?

Over the years, I have discovered many other pearls of wisdom. Usually they come from attending a seminar or reading an inspirational book. One of my favorites is: "If I can take just one great idea away from this and use it, the time and price will be well worth the cost." I forget who first said this, but it is still lodged in my mind. Some other memorable quotes: "If this were your company, what would you do?" and "That's history. Forget it." I do remember who said these—former managers who mentored me early in my career. I treasure their memory.

To a degree, we are all products of our past experiences and our future aspirations. We live out our lives as the center-point marker on the rope in a tug of war, first pulled one way and then the other—until we reach a point where we commit either to focus on our past experiences or strive to create grander new ones. It all comes down to who or what owns your future. Is it your past? Your memories? Your habits? Your history? Or will it be your ambition that creates your bigger future? Comfort or creation? It is always yours to choose. Either your future dreams or your past experiences will influence where your tomorrows will take you. This is the whole point of this book. Who is going to own your future? You or someone else?

I have attended many workshops, and read hundreds of books. The more great ideas I encountered, the harder it became to choose which ones to implement. I discovered that I could achieve an inspirational "high" just by showing up. But I did not want to become a "self-help junkie" floating from one inspirational event to the next, ever searching for the right message to lead me to the promised land of self-improved bliss.

I knew that I could not live off the ideas of others. Personal improvement is never a spectator sport. I had to enter the playing field myself. I had to create goals—truly exciting goals involving my imagination and reflecting my life's purpose. Through my goals I would create my future and I would take possession of it. The goals that I set for myself determine that I want to own my future.

I have always been concerned that, even after pursuing a career for ten years, I would wake up one day and realize that I had gained only one year's worth of experience and repeated it ten times, rather than growing from my compounded experiences. I want to add value in exchange for the space I occupy on this earth. *Hey! I Can Do This* is the result of this motivation.

Whether you consider each moment of living as a precious gift or you are convinced that this life is just a dress rehearsal, you will gain valuable insights from this book. It approaches goals differently than any of the hundreds on the market. By following the ideas and exercises here, you will inspire yourself to instill new passion into your life and seek higher highs than ever before. The tools introduced here will turbocharge you to *go beyond the limits of having too much information and not enough passion to act.*

Throughout this book, there are several opportunities for you to gather your thoughts. These have all been included with a purpose. Specifically, you will develop your action plan—a place to start and a method to follow when applying the great ideas that inspire you. You will clarify what is important to you and why. You will organize your priorities and you will take purposeful action as never before. In short, your answer to the question "Who owns your future?" will be "I do!" This will lead you to achieve what you truly want.

To your success!

Introduction

We all set goals. We all struggle to achieve them.

How many times have you looked back at the end of a busy day only to realize that you have not accomplished any of the things you had planned to? You know that you were busy! You probably even focused on what seemed like your highest priority throughout the day, but it is easy to mis-prioritize objectives and focus on low-priority projects that do not contribute to your most important goals. If you are like many people, this is a regular occurrence. Eventually, a deluge of *real* high-priority activities dramatically drops on you. This is when you face the ancient dilemma of whether you should drain the swamp or beat off the alligators.

These "alligators" are not restricted by age or gender. For students, they can be assignments that are coming due. For career employees—that quarterly report. For stay-at-home spouses, there are end-of-summer, back-to-school preparations and Thanks-giving dinners to plan. For those in the 50-plus group, their pending retirement can be one of those alligators lurking in the depths.

Regardless of your age, the educational or employment work-place that formally structures your daily activities can suddenly disappear. The lucky ones welcome these changes; however, many people face career change with regret; some see it as mark-ing not only the loss of structure but also the loss of friendships, purpose, and meaning. The financial planner in me says that it is not having adequately prepared for their future that can leave them ill-equipped for the demands of their next life stage of financial independence.

So how can you beat off these alligators while draining the swamp too? How do you create a life with purpose that adds excitement and vigor to each and every day?

Adopt an attitude of life-long goal achievement—be constantly learning and doing. Seek out new experiences and learn new skills not only during your formal education years, but throughout your working years and the many years that a productive retirement will offer.

I believe that setting goals and achieving them are the best ways to accomplish this. There is no age limit on goal setting and goal achievement.

Many of the goals that we want—good health, peace of mind, loving family relationships—are shared by all. Yet having common issues does not automatically lead to using the same solutions. Each person's view of the same issue may be defined differently. The basic issue itself can be as multifaceted as a diamond. Finding a solution not only requires understanding the problem, but also determining the context in which the problem must be solved. "Context" includes your strengths and weaknesses, your resources and time frames, your personal stage in life, and many other factors. These factors may complicate matters, but they also provide subtle nuances that make the problems—and their solutions—uniquely yours.

Although my orientation comes from my experience as a financial planner, this is not a book about finance. It is about you and the priceless benefits you will receive by achieving goals that are meaningful to you—planning and living your life the way you want to, and achieving the dreams that are *your* dreams.

I regularly speak with my clients about their dreams and goals. Whether it is buying a house, retiring early, helping their children finance their education, starting a business, cruising around the world, or contributing to a worthy cause, their goals have two things in common. The goals are always important to them and they are always about what the money can buy—never just about the money. Being a financial planner is about helping people achieve their goals and make their dreams come true.

Financial planning provides me with a disciplined, future-oriented mind-set to observe, identify, group, and develop an understanding of regularly repeating patterns. I have observed that, although each of us is unique, when we are thinking about our biggest dreams or deepest concerns, most of these generally fit into one of several common "big pictures."

You might think, "Hey, just a minute! Your clients' goals are like the ones I have! What about world peace? A cure for cancer? Ending global poverty or AIDS?" These big-picture goals need your attention, too. Just remember the words of the airline attendant: "If the airbag drops down, put yours on first, then help others around you." It is always up to you. You decide when your goals are taken care of and you are in a position to help others.

Warning: This book's purpose is to help you maximize your opportunity to assess where you have come from, where you are now, where you are going, and whether you are on the right path. This way you can be the proactive sculptor of your own destiny.

No matter how busy you are, taking small steps to consciously choose the future you want will reward you with confidence, accomplishment, and satisfaction. Having a purpose and a plan makes the difference between enjoying the trip and simply going along for the ride. In the words of Lewis Carroll's famous Cheshire Cat, "If you don't know where you're going, any road will get you there."

It is your turn to choose the road to your desired goals and move forward with a new understanding—focusing your priorities and shaping your destiny. When you come to your fork in the road, you will choose the best route with confidence. You will know it leads where you want to go!

Focus is key. There are many focusing exercises in this book. By completing them, you will gain new insight into your life priorities. Not only will you develop your vision; you will also create the future you desire—on purpose. *Hey! I Can Do This* introduces a new paradigm: "The Living on Purpose Paradigm." The following is a brief summary of the journey you are embarking upon.

The Road Map For The Living On Purpose Paradigm

The Living on Purpose Paradigm has three tenets:

1. You can achieve just about anything that you set your mind to and actively work towards achieving.

2. You need a feedback system to move you progressively towards your desired outcomes.

3. What you do in one area of your life is dynamic and affects other areas of your life.

The Living on Purpose Paradigm provides both a strategy and a system to accomplish your goals. There are lots of exercises and worksheets to develop and expand your thoughts. As you work through this book, you will develop and expand your goal setting and goal achievement ideas into meaningful and useable elements. You can print off these exercise templates in a "fill-in-able" format at **www.HeyIcandoThis.com.**

I promise these elements will make sense to you. The result: you will create a dynamic, values-based process that maximizes your assets, helps you achieve your goals, and improves your quality of life.

One more point: I have never been a big fan of using a $5.00 word when a 50¢ word will do. You may notice that sometimes the 50¢ word will be used in a context slightly different from common usage. In this case, please read for deeper understanding and allow for a few instances where you might have to say "Okay, in this exercise, this word is being used to convey this meaning." I am sure that you will prefer this in place of specialized jargon, and as a result find the exercises more meaningful and enjoyable.

Here is an example of what I mean: consider the word *priority*. You probably know your highest priority. Right? Usually, it is what you consider most important in your life and where you want to focus your time and effort. Now, if you look back over the past 24 or 48 hours, what did you actually spend the bulk of your time and your greatest effort doing? In terms of actual time spent, if this time was not focused upon your greatest *theoretical priority*, it was spent on your greatest *actual* priority. So the question might be, "Does your theoretical priority match your actual priority?"

You can do this!

Here is what to expect as you move forward.

Part One—Setting The Context For Change looks at what makes you feel alive, and deals with theory, background, and definitions. You learn about the five quotients of the Whole Person Concept and how these create your values. The Whole Person Concept is an idea that I am sure you will find interesting. You will see how your values help you develop your goals. This background will provide a solid foundation in setting meaningful goals.

Part Two—Activating Your "Whole Person" - these basics help you develop the framework to achieve your goals by introducing two individual tools critical to your goal achievement—the Goals Incubator and the Tactical Goal Achievement Process.

Part Three—Goal Setting And Goal Achieving enables you to define what is most important to you and to set meaningful goals. With the help of worksheets and illustrations, you will analyze your own place in life while examining the five Whole Person Concept's quotients and developing clear goals based upon your values.

Part Four—Activating The Paradigm taps into methods and resources that help crystallize the paradigm model and lead to living your life on purpose. This section also introduces two major tools: the 90-Day Follow-up Strategy and the Major Goals Momentum System. We will also look at your habits as your own personal best practices.

Part Five—Pulling It All Together helps you avoid pitfalls when developing your new skills and creating new habits that support your goals as you bring all the components together. Taking ownership of your future and even personal reincarnation are covered.

You will find that applying these paradigm principles is like participating in an interactive workshop. At times, you may feel challenged in putting pen to paper in a way that fully satisfies you. Do not let this alarm you; it is natural to have difficulty beginning this process. *The most important thing is to start and see it through.* Take time to think, rethink, articulate, work, and rework your answers on paper until they are crystal clear. With this insight, you will confidently move forward—with purpose.

This book will open your eyes and mind to your greatest potential.

Be prepared to commit to:

★ Defining your vision from your passion

★ Being willing to experiment, take risks, and endure a little discomfort

★ Taking action toward making your dreams come true

All of your hard work in setting and achieving your most meaningful goals will be rewarded through living according to your highest priorities and progressively creating the grandest future that you are committed to attaining.

PART ONE

Setting The Context For Change

What man actually needs is not a tensionless state but rather the striving and struggling for some goal worthy of him. What he needs is not the discharge of tension at any cost, but the call of a potential meaning waiting to be fulfilled by him.

—Victor Frankl (1905-1997)
Psychiatrist and Holocaust Survivor[1]

Victor Frankl attributed his surviving the Holocaust in part to his realization that, inwardly, he always had control over how he chose to respond to the atrocities that he witnessed and to which he was subjected. This helped him keep meaning in his life and stay alive. Hopefully, you may never have to test yourself in such a manner.

[1] Viktor E. Frankl, *Man's Search for Meaning.* Copyright © 1959, 1962, 1984, 1992 by Viktor E. Frankl. Reprinted by permission of Beacon Press, Boston.

.

Moving Forward:
What Makes You Truly Feel Alive?

What gives you that tingling sense of striving and experiencing being alive?

Are you a kinesthetic person? Muscles stretching and flexing, working up a good sweat. The feel of the wind in your face and against your body. Diving into ice-cold lake water at dawn or nestling into a bubbling hot tub at dusk.

Do you get revved up when you are in a social setting, being part of the crowd? Meeting and greeting? Leading the crowd? Are you the life of the party?

Is it the familiarity of family—loved ones whom you have known forever? You know what they are going to say before they say it and they know just as much about you. It is warm and comforting.

Making the sale...putting it all on the line—what could be more satisfying for some of us than closing the big one, receiving that career promotion or large bonus check?

Do you thrill to pure sensuality? The slick softness of your cat's fur, the feel of a silk camisole against your skin...a caress...making love?

How about buying something expensive to add to your stable of possessions—or giving it all away to someone who needs it more than you? Contributing to a cause you believe in beyond all else? Standing up and being counted?

Do you delight in food—not *food*—but **FOOD**—the aroma, the taste, the texture? A gourmet presentation. Savor it! (Makes your mouth water just thing about it!) Is this where you get your maximum sense of being?

Do smiles open your heart? That of your six-week-old baby, so innocent, so dependent, so all-accepting…of your elderly mother as you arrive for a visit that takes the silence from her home…of your perfect life mate when she takes your breath away with her beauty and allure.

Earning the big bucks! Selling the stock at the top! Lottery wins! Las Vegas—no, somewhere grander—Monte Carlo! Here I come!

Passing the test! Making the team! Closing the deal! Hearing the applause!

Do sounds exceptionally move you? The call of a loon across the still waters of a northern lake at sunset…the thundering roar of the surf hitting the tropical island's shore or the trickle of the babbling brook in the emerald green forest. The swoosh of the golf club as it makes precise contact with the ball…the whispering voice of that special someone.

The melody of a song carrying memories from your past…a classic rhapsody from Gershwin, or a famous operatic piece such as "Nessun Dorma" or the "Pilgrim's Chorus" from *Tannhauser*…"The Ride of the Valkyries"…oldies by the Beatles, the Beach Boys, Bob Dylan…country hits by Faith Hill and Lee Ann Womack…the national anthem…played in your honor.

Everyone is different.

As you read the above examples, there were those you looked at and said, "Oh ya! I know just what you mean," and there were those that left you feeling less than lukewarm—feeling like you had just picked up cold, limp spaghetti…or maybe a handful of worms.

The thing is, one person needs to win an election to get the same feeling that another gets by being part of a winning team, or by cheering for a horse in the Derby, or by watching a son or daughter receive special honors…or that comes with the "Eureka moment" of discovering a major scientific breakthrough, or adding that special postage stamp or rare coin or comic book (I mean graphic novel) to your collection…or after twenty years of dead-ended research, finally making the link that takes your family tree back one more generation…or seeing championship blue ribbons in your new pedigree puppy's eyes.

We are all different and yet we are all the same.

We want to feel alive. We want to feel that special value is created by our efforts.

We want the experiences—physical, sensual, social, intellectual, financial, spiritual—that take us to a special place of "me-ness" that we would like to return to again and again.

The question is, "How do you get what you want?" It seems like it would be pretty simple, yet most of us spend huge amounts of time and money in the quest of getting what we want. Then when we do get it, many of us do not seem to enjoy it! Is it the quest for the novel, the unfamiliar, the unattainable? Is it that the familiar holds less value than the unknown? Maybe….Perhaps it is because we often do not know what we want, or once we finally attain something, we do not remember why we wanted it in the first place! The former sense of fulfillment is missing. We discover that it is either time to raise the bar—or go to a bar and rethink our priorities.

The bottom line is that to feel more alive, more passionate, more in tune with yourself, your aspirations, and your inspirations, you need to do, have, and experience more of whatever it is that makes you feel most alive. This should become your goal. This is the "pleasure" half of the Pleasure–Pain Principle—seeking pleasure and avoiding pain. If the Pleasure–Pain Principle is new to you, it refers to the natural tendency to seek more of what pleases you and less of what you find painful. These are both basic motivators. One pulls you towards what you desire and want more of (i.e., praise, recognition, or comfort); the other pushes you away from what hurts you and what you will go to great lengths to avoid (i.e., physical pain, failure or ridicule). The reality is that whether you are goal oriented or not, and regardless of how much sense this simple idea may make to you, most people let other, less important distractions keep them from what they desire most. Is this done on purpose? Not likely! Can this be done without thinking? Most definitely yes!

I hope that reading this chapter has stimulated your imagination. You have found yourself thinking back, visualizing the "who, what, where, when, why, and hows" of your greatest passions and enjoyment in your life. You are realizing that—if it has been missing in your life—like an old friend the pleasure of passionate moments can return to you.

Go ahead! Let your passions awaken your purpose!

Get some paper and a pen. Start by making a list of your greatest passions, your greatest desires—and do not think too much about it. Instead, *feel* that excitement, that desire, that passion! Write it all down—in a breathless rush if you have to—without editorial comment or judgment. You just might surprise yourself! (Yes, I promised you there would be many self-exploratory exercises to stimulate your goal setting muscles. This is the first one. Go for it!)

You are embarking upon a journey of self-discovery. As you progress, you will become increasingly more effective at articulating what you want in life and what you are prepared to do to attain it. The objective is to help you realize that your goals are attainable and that once you have achieved a goal, it is time to enjoy it.

We are going to get a little introspective in some parts and analytical in others. There will be some problem solving and some list making. You might even find yourself asking, "Why do I want this?" Well, that is the whole idea. As life becomes more complicated, you can lose touch with your basic preferences and motivations. Your focus can drift away from what you want…to what you think you want…to what should get you closer to what you want…to what someone else tells you that you should want.

It is time to get back to the basics… to your passions—your dreams and goals—and to progress according to your preferences. When your goals fill your life with accomplishments that make you feel alive, you look forward to each day's newness, anticipating the pleasurable experiences. Part of the newness comes from curiosity and the opportunity to find out what would happen *if*…. Part comes from your desire to experience more pleasure and avoid pain.

∞

At a basic level, the first goals you set relate to the earliest, simplest pleasures in life. As a baby, you suckle milk for nourishment. It relieves your hunger. It gives you warmth and comfort. When you want more (one of the first and fundamental goal-setting experiences), you communicate—boy, can you communicate!—and your goal is fulfilled. As you grow older, you raise the bar. Your goals become refined and you become harder to please. Much of your life becomes a quest for goal satisfaction. As you gain more experiences, you continue to raise the bar. You refine your expectations and the quest evolves to an ever-advancing higher level of complexity—until something changes and you start to lower the bar once again.

What might cause you to set lower goals? Sometimes it is necessary to purposely lower your expectations. This would be the case when learning a new skill or recuperating from a serious illness. But once you have mastered the basic level, you will want the challenge of achieving greater goals. Unthinkingly lowering the bar, however, is a tragedy. For whatever reason, you may start to settle for less and less—and less—and your future slowly evolves into your past. You lose interest in your tomorrows and in growing. With nothing to look forward to, you begin to die a little bit every day. Although growth and decay are natural, giving up is not. It is part of human nature to continually focus and strive for the next improvement—no matter how small. You need this to expand your capabilities, to create a bigger future for yourself. Through aging or illness, your capabilities may contract;

however, you can still have expectations greater than your current capabilities permit, and move beyond those capabilities to reach your next bigger future. Regardless of your current capabilities, even your most grandiose goals require step-by-step blueprint-level action to be accomplished. There is no fairy dust that will turn the "98-pound weakling into Mr. Hercules." It all comes down to working a workable plan. (Remember what I said earlier about words taking on an uncommon meaning? This might be one of those times.)

It is most important that you have goals that create momentum in your life. If you are new to goal setting, know that achieving your goal is all about changing your life. Your goal is yours, not someone else's. Another person's "realistic" goal might be your "optimistic" goal. If it is *your* goal, then that is where you start. Progress will come. The important thing is to get started, to create a sense of momentum. For some, your goal might be to create a new habit that you will practice every day. For others, "every day" can sound like "forever"…maybe you need a compromise…what if you did it for just a few days or a week?…maybe then another…and build a streak of consecutive days. Gradually momentum can generate a change in preference and your new habit is born.

Even in goal setting and goal striving, "life happens." Roadblocks appear that can knock you off your horse. Idealism meets realism. Realistic goals—based upon your current capabilities—can serve as a starting point to help you gain momentum. Because of illness, age, or refocusing of interests, your capabilities may have diminished. It is easy to get discouraged after a life-altering event such as a stroke or heart attack….when formerly simple tasks become major challenges. Setting 'realistic goals" in this type of situation will move you forward. After all, no one knows what is your "realistic" and what is your "reach out for the stars" for you—but you.

As you grow older, changing your interests is just as natural as the awareness and the curiosity that helped to shape them in the first place. Realistic goals require that you take a good look at yourself to establish your next target and create an action plan to increase your capabilities and widen your future.

Then you just go out and do it!

This is working your workable plan.

Get Proactive!

It is said that whatever you measure will improve. So, when you focus on proactively creating a bigger future, you introduce and track subtle nuances of expectation and fulfillment into your life. These keep you fresh and "in the game." For maximum enjoyment, even the top golf pros need to find greater challenges to stay sharp in every game—at their competitive peak and long after.

Chapter 1
Why Set Goals In The First Place?

All life's happiness comes from achieving goals. When you look back on your life, what will make you happy will be the great thing you have done, the superb family you raised, the prosperous business you created, the places you traveled to and the exciting books you have read. You'll not look back and find a sense of accomplishment in the television shows you watched or in the weekend mornings that you slept until noon. Your life will be elevated by one thing and one thing alone: achievement. This doesn't mean that you must strive to make 10 million dollars or build a home in Bermuda. Achievement and life success can appear in peace of mind and a well-developed spiritual life. The key is simply to achieve. Discipline and will power will make you a success.

—Robin Sharma[2]

It is the accomplishment, not the preparation, that you will remember. There is a strong connection between happiness in life and the achievement of goals that are meaningful to you. Each time an important goal is achieved, you raise the bar. The completed goal becomes a stepping-stone, part of the process towards achieving a higher goal. When you look back at your major goal's successful achievement, the stepping-stones of your accomplishments stretch out in a line. It is interesting that if you look at a straight line under a high level of magnification, it becomes a series of dots—just like your stepping-stones. In the same way,

[2] Robin Sharma, *Mega Living! Powerful Wisdom for Self-Leadership.* Toronto: The Haunsla Corp., 2004, pp. 28-29.

each minor goal becomes part of the process towards a greater goal. Your greater goal!

Yet, for most of us, days fly by without any significant progress toward the achievement of our current goals. We forget about the cumulative importance of each day's stepping-stones. We say that we will have time to work on them…tomorrow. We know that they are important. We know that our goals "fire us up." But, for most, the demands of today get in the way and "tomorrow" never comes. The point is that the best time to work on our key goals in life is always…*right now*.

We need to keep our greater goal more visible and more memorable so that we can see how each stepping-stone goal leads us ever closer to the higher goal. This grander goal needs to capture our imagination so that it does not get derailed by lesser distractions.

In about 350 B.C., the philosopher Aristotle said it this way:

First, have a definite, clear practical ideal, a goal, an objective.

Second, have the necessary means to achieve your ends: wisdom, money, materials and methods.

Third, adjust all your means to that end.

To me, the Aristotle quote sums up much of what we need to do to be successful. Obviously, the world has changed over the past 2000+ years, but the simple wisdom remains. Table 1 gives Aristotle a 21st-century twist.

Table 1: Quotes Comparison

Aristotle's 350-B.C. Perspective	My 21st-Century Perspective
"First, have a definite, clear practical ideal, a goal, an objective."	**Focus:** Focusing clearly on your goal—knowing what you want to do.
"Second, have the necessary means to achieve your ends: wisdom, money, materials, and methods."	**Empowerment:** Having *all* the tools—yes, all the tools—needed to achieve your goal—no excuses.
"Third, adjust all your means to that end."	**Persistence:** Remembering what is most important to you and why, and taking *repeated* action.

We will be coming back to this simple idea many times as you read on. First you need to focus on your goal. Next, you need the key resources necessary to achieve your goal. Then you need to consistently apply your resources toward achieving your goal.

With this perspective in mind, let's do a quick experiment to determine how this applies. Let me ask you two questions. I call them "The Mind-Stretcher Questions." Think back to three years ago and ask yourself the following:

If you had known you could never fail, what three goals would you have focused on over the past three years?

Take a moment to reflect. Write down your answers in the space below (Exercise 1).

There is no trick here, no limits on what you could choose. Open your mind to all the possibilities that you have ever considered. Think beyond any physical, financial, attitudinal, social, or educational limitations that you see as roadblocks. If need be, see yourself winning the lottery or married to the president of the company. It is your life and your dream, so take the time to think about your biggest dreams—benefit from your hindsight.

NOTE: Exercise 1 is illustrated here for your reference as a "non-fill-in-able" form. As mentioned in the Introduction, "full-size" exercise templates are available at the companion website **www.HeyIcandoThis.com**.

Exercise 1: Mind-Stretcher Question-Past Three Years

If you had known you could never fail, what three goals would you have focused on over the past three years?

1._____

2._____

3._____

Great! You have listed three goals that are very important to you. But how important? Did you achieve them? Could you have done better?

Now, next to each of these goals, write down what slowed you down or stopped you from achieving it. Do you see the "make it or break it" importance of "keeping your goal top of mind?" If you had kept your goal prominent in your mind and your actions, the outcome would have been different. This is where either the "Empowerment" or "Persistence" dimension usually breaks down.

Okay, take a deep breath. Put the past behind you. Now think about your biggest, best possible future. Here is the second question:

If your success were guaranteed, what three goals would you strive to achieve over the next three years?

Take a moment. Challenge yourself. Detail your answers in Exercise 2.

Exercise 2: Mind-Stretcher Question-Next Three Years

If your success were guaranteed, what three goals would you strive to achieve over the next three years?

1._____

2._____

3._____

Now, next to each goal, write down the main obstacle you will most likely need to overcome to achieve it. (In doing this, you are anticipating your roadblocks to success and you can plan actions to bring you closer to your goals. This will help you empower yourself to achieve your goal.)

The first question awakened your mind; this second one sets

up new possibilities. *Whatever you write down is the correct answer.* It sets your direction. When your goal is clear, whatever you do to "make it happen" is consistent with your vision. When your actions move you towards your most important goals, you are living on purpose and moving towards the future that you want to create. Of course, you have obstacles to overcome, and in many instances you already know what they are. Your personal resolve is to achieve your goal—on purpose.

When you live "on purpose" you are focused on achieving your clear, definite goal.

You may not remember your earliest goal-achieving experiences, but you demonstrated great conviction in your ability to live on purpose when, as a toddler, you struggled to learn how to walk. Why did you set this goal? Because everyone else was walking! You wanted to walk, too. Regardless of the obstacles, no matter how many times you fell, you kept at it until you mastered the art of walking. Then you raised your goal and started running!

You have demonstrated similar determination many other times in your life. What about your first attempts at talking? You made all the sounds necessary and *you* knew what they were supposed to mean. After all, you had heard big people making these same sounds your whole life. Do you remember how happy you felt when that big person was finally smart enough to understand what you were saying? That person's praise reinforced your determination. *You* knew what you wanted. *You* knew how to get it. From your perspective, everyone else was just a little "developmentally challenged"!

Being Goal Focused, Not Goal Driven

Living on purpose is more about being *goal focused* rather than *goal driven*. By understanding certain concepts and applying them consistently, you can define and achieve your biggest dreams. As our old buddy Aristotle pointed out, you have to adjust all your means to that end and keep working at it. The demands of simply getting through the day can get in the way of goal achievement. Persistence becomes a tool to keep you working at your goals.

Hey! I Can Do This is your ticket to goal achievement. The exercises you will complete are the stepping-stones on your path towards self-actualization. You will identify your top goals in each of five key areas: financial, physical, spiritual, intellectual, and social. You will:

* ★ Decide on the specific next steps to move forward for each goal
* ★ Establish a timetable to achieve the next phase of each goal you set
* ★ Develop a follow-up and feedback mechanism that works for you
* ★ Monitor and evaluate your progress
* ★ Achieve and maintain a balance while continuing to move towards your goals

Why Your Goals Get Sidetracked

Let's conduct a brief experiment to demonstrate how your brain focuses on information. Here is your first test:

Clear your mind. Ready?

Try not to think about an orange!

The color, the texture, the taste, the smell. It is virtually impossible to not think about an orange for at least the first tenth of a second. Regardless of my request that you not focus on an orange, automatically (subconsciously) you did until your conscious mind took over. Subconsciously, you responded to an idea of what orange means to you. Be honest! You are probably swallowing right now because this image is making you salivate!

Let's try again.

Clear your mind. Ready?

Try *not* to think about an elephant and a zebra!

Did you visualize one or the other? Both? Neither? A striped elephant? A zebra with huge ears? Psychologists know that it is harder to think about two different things at the same time. When you successfully think about multiple items, they require context to connect them to each other.

The point here is that in real life, you only think about one thing at a time. You are regularly shifting your attention (and your actions) from one priority to another. Regardless of its importance, when you get distracted and an immediate concern grabs your attention, it becomes your "top priority of the moment."

The question is, How do you get back to focusing on what is most important to you—your true top priority?

Your Priority Oasis-The Reset Button

With so many diverse demands pulling and pushing at you, prioritizing your time takes on a whole new dimension. It is easy to get sidetracked and let your high-priority goals slip to a lower priority. Being interested and getting distracted is a daily fact of life. What is your strategy to get you back on track? You need a "Reset Button" that you can push to snap you back to your top priorities. (We have a secret process for this, which will be revealed in a later chapter.) Whenever you are distracted, *just press your Priority Reset Button.* Review your priorities. In doing so, you are actually holding a personal "mini-goal review" to refocus on the priority most important to you. These mini-goal reviews will become your "Priority Oasis"—a time and place to regroup, refresh, and reconfirm your top priorities. There, you reestablish your balance by keeping your goals focused, integrated, and congruent. As a side benefit, you will see a synergy develop among your goals in different areas of your life. You will discover that activities leading you towards one goal will extend their benefits towards other goals as well. (More about this in Chapter 11.) Tapping into your goal reset process includes the following:

★ Reviewing your motivation, level of commitment, and existing resources that relate to the goal

★ Knowing where to find—and how to tap into—new and existing resources

★ Establishing the next steps to move you towards your goal and keeping you on track

★ Adopting a system that consistently brings you back to your priorities

Hit that Reset Button now! Get ready for a boost in how to live your life on purpose!

Chapter 2
Learning To Live On Purpose

As you awaken each day,
the world offers you another 24 hours in which to do your best.
1440 precious minutes.
Another 86,400 seconds will pass before the sun is in its same
position tomorrow.
How will you use your most precious and irreplaceable asset?
Sleep commands 6 to 8 hours. This first 26,400 of your daily
allotment of seconds recharges your body and your mind. The other
60,000 are yours to spend as you choose.
Some spend their seconds complaining,
others compose rhapsodies,
some wage war,
others strive for harmony, understanding, and world peace.
Each day think of the highest possible use for your 60,000 seconds.
Create purpose in your life.
Use today's 60,000 to build on yesterday's and to prepare for
tomorrow's allotment.
Each day, a gift to you—86,400 precious seconds—
part for your body and part to leave your mark on the world.
Will you leave graffiti or a timeless masterpiece for all to marvel?
Live your best life brilliantly.
Do your best work.
*Create the best future **you**.*
Leave the best for those you love
and who love you.

Each person has a role to play and a contribution to make. There are no bit parts. Every person's role is significant. It is just that sometimes your significance escapes your view.

When you think of great people who lived "large," or have demonstrated a singleness of purpose and achieved wonderful things, names like Thomas Edison, Mother Theresa and Nelson Mandela come to mind. All were leaders of great conviction, passion, commitment, and vision. They were known for living "on purpose." Yet, none of their special attributes developed in a vacuum. Rather, their habits developed through the influence of their own personal role models and mentors.

Think about it. Every Einstein starts out by learning something important to his or her future success from someone else—someone who helped the novice to develop curiosity or confidence, and who enabled the budding genius to focus on his or her passion.

Could you be next? You may never know your own "purpose in life" unequivocally, but you can bet that you have one. Are you the next great scientist, leader, inventor? Perhaps you are a fabulous parent, teacher, coach, neighbor, aunt, or grandparent who inspires greatness in others. How will you know when it is your turn to demonstrate brilliance? Most people will never know, but opportunities have appeared and more will. The future leaders who benefit from your wisdom and perspective will know and be forever in your debt. You will not gain this insight by reading your horoscope. It is more likely that the opportunity will find *you*.

If you knew in your heart that from this day forward your actions would influence the course of history, would you change the way you live each day? Would you watch less TV? Exercise more? Laugh more? Pray more? Contribute more? Whatever your answer, you can make the world better than you found it—anticipate purpose in your life!

Purpose is a curious word. For many, *purpose* represents a spiritual quest—a search for meaning and value in life by seeking out God's reason for placing them on earth and defining their mission in life. Others define *purpose* as how they will add value to the world before they die. Regardless of which is your source of inspirational passion, it will lead you towards similar goals and outwardly visible results. Either way, the more you act on purpose, the more your life becomes filled with the added momentum of purpose.

Each and every day, you do "things." These "things" lead you towards the goal that you most purposefully want to achieve. Although you would like to say that you act with intention, often you may find that this is not the case. You are performing many of your activities either by habit or by accident. Perhaps you even find that on many occasions, either you do not believe in, or you are not aware of, the potential outcomes of your actions. It is fundamental that you accept the results of your actions whether you purposefully intend them or not.

In this book, then, *purpose* means "willingly done with intention." When you want to do something on purpose, you set goals and you create strategies to achieve them. You act according to your best intentions; however, your habits and daily living can still get in the way.

So, what *can* you do to identify your purpose?

Why not start with your greatest passions? Why not live every day with the expectation that today it is your turn to be brilliant—*knowing that, every day, you are helping to shape the future of humankind?* After all, you come from a long line of survivors. Your parents, their parents, and all your ancestors were survivors. More than that, they were contributors, educators, and role models who helped create the person you are and the world you live in. Now it is your turn to fill your life with passion—with a sense of aliveness—as you use your assets and resources to make your contribution to the future!

Take Hold Of Your Future

As mentioned earlier, you first discovered that you could do things "on purpose" as a child. This was around the time you learned about "cause and effect" or "stimulus and response." Consider the following situation and recall similar ones in your childhood:

Mary and Billy are playing in the sandbox.

Mary fills her pail with sand.

Mary looks at Billy.

Billy is playing happily with a truck.

Mary stands up with her pail full of sand.

She walks over to Billy and dumps it over his head.

Billy starts to cry and shouts, "You did that on purpose!"

Mary shouts back, "I did not!...It was...an accident!"

Like Mary, you may have experienced unanticipated results and learned to avoid taking responsibility for doing things "on purpose." You may have learned to see the undesirable aspects of accountability disappear when your behavior becomes "accidental." Over time, this resistance to being accountable can become a learned behavior and it can be carried into adulthood. Gradually your focus can even shift from being personally accountable, to assuming someone else is. Do you see how this habit can work against you?

Like so many others, you work hard to develop the techniques and capabilities necessary for skill and career advancement. However, when complimented on your accomplishments, do you modestly downplay your special characteristics and your extreme effort to develop them? How often have you heard others minimize their significance by saying, "It was nothing..." when they really wanted to say, "Thank you, I'm glad you noticed. Ya' know, I've been working to improve that skill for the past five years!"

Have you ever considered that you can create your future in advance…that you can groom yourself for the future you want? You do not suddenly wake up one day as a completely new person. So it must be that day by day, you create little pieces of the person you become—whether it is couch potato, Olympic athlete, casual laborer, or best-selling author—the person that you grow into is the person that you create. You get to choose whether to create this person on purpose or by accident—but in either case, the person you turn into is the result of the actions or inactions that you take now. Your actions are the confirmation of your decision.

So how do you create your future in advance? You decide what you want. You decide what you are willing to pay for it. You live your life "on purpose." For example, when asked about the secret of his or her success, just about every star athlete refers to the hours of extra practice devoted to perfecting a key, critically differentiating skill. It is through the doing of more than what is expected, and doing it with a passion… that "doing" creates the difference. To find out how this applies to you, keep reading!

Doing things "on purpose" is liberating. When you act on purpose, you do it for a reason. But when you do not do something on purpose, how do you know why you did it? Perhaps it is because:

★ Someone told you to

★ You did it by accident

★ It was a reflex action

★ It seemed like a good idea at the time

★ You weren't thinking about what you were doing

★ You wanted to see what the outcome would be

★ You didn't expect the outcome of your action to turn out the way it did

★ You were distracted and meant to do something else

★ It was just a habit, so ingrained that you didn't recognize doing it

This list just sounds like a bunch of excuses, doesn't it?

In contrast, when you live "on purpose" and something goes wrong, you have collected new information. You *know* what went wrong. You *know* what you did to cause the negative result. You *know* you cannot shift the blame to anyone else. You did it! You created the outcome. Remember, when something does not go according to plan, it does not make *you* a failure. It just means you have more information to use in the future as you seek different, preferable results. Your life is an exercise in collecting information and learning from it.

Accountability should apply when things go right, too! When you successfully achieve a goal, accept the praise. *You did it*. You deserve the recognition for your achievements. You deserve the opportunity to decide whether and how you will replicate your success.

Live In The Moment To Live On Purpose

Whenever you do something on purpose, you are living in the moment. You are experiencing and learning, actively and immediately. Your intent and your freedom to act are part of what makes you uniquely "you," free to act or not to act. You are also:

★ Working towards one of your top priorities in your life

★ Focusing on your goals and actively taking them to their next levels

★ No longer living by accident

Can someone skydive "by accident"? Not normally. Although skydiving remains outside my personal comfort level, I suspect that most people who jump out of airplanes do so "on purpose" and do it for the exhilarating sense of being alive that it gives them. But the most successful ones do it only after taking safety precautions to maximize the thrill of the moment and minimize the likelihood of a serious mishap. In skydiving, errors can be fatal!

Can you live "on purpose" all the time? That is the ideal, but with so many different demands pulling at you, it is difficult. However, when you prioritize your activities based on your committed goals, you are living "on purpose." *You know the "why" behind the "what" that you do each day.*

If the idea of living on purpose is new, you should sneak up on it by doing a little at a time. Gradually increase the number of purpose-focused activities you pursue. Life is full of the consequences of your past decisions. In many instances, it may not be practical to suddenly turn your back on past commitments. You can, however, still see them through to completion after adopting your new perspective.

Start by focusing on one goal. Gradually build to a higher level of goal setting rather than attacking several purpose-filled goals at once. (We will get much more into the topic of goal setting in later chapters.)

Influencing Outcomes

Do you believe that when you take action, there can be a predictable result—a cause and an effect? I do. I believe that whenever you do something on purpose, you *seek* a particular result. You choose one action over all other possibilities because of that desired outcome. Where you know danger lurks, you mitigate your risk by taking precautions—like our skydiver does.

On the other hand, because you have free will, you are free to do whatever you choose. You can choose to ignore conventional logic, to throw caution to the wind, and to take action regardless of the risk—like maintaining a lifelong cigarette smoking habit or failing to check the length of the bungee cord. Either way, you are acting on purpose and with purpose. You are choosing and influencing the outcome that your actions are most likely to create.

How do skydivers influence the future outcome of their

skydives? With study and practice, they strive to improve the experience and lower their risk. For example, before every dive, they complete a proven checklist of activities. Some items are mandatory while others are voluntary. They learn the processes, techniques, and habits from a teacher or coach who has helped others become successful. Taken together, these activities form a "checklist for successful skydiving" and they influence the outcomes. (There might even be a lucky rabbit's foot listed somewhere on the checklist!) Similarly, using a success checklist helps ensure the purposeful and positive achievement of any goal you set.

"Newness"—Keeping The Spark Alive

You may remember specific instances of living on purpose—events that occurred only in certain areas of your life and only at specific times. Remember how you felt just as your wedding ceremony began? You were marrying the most perfect, most desirable person ever to enter into your life to marry you—if you have not done it yet, imagine how it will feel! The tingling...the hope...the uncertainty...the fear...the euphoria! (This is about as specific as one can get to acting on purpose and attempting to influence an outcome.)

Then comes the hard part—keeping the original spark alive, in spite of the passage of time. Gradually, habits are formed to replace the "newness" of first-time experience with the predictable repetitiveness of the familiar. Sometimes this is helpful, such as when driving a car. Sometimes habitually relying on predictability can be counterproductive, such as when nurturing a cherished relationship. How do you ensure that your original intent does not fall victim to habit? How do you ensure that you do not lose interest and replace your original living-on-purpose intent with a living-by-accident outcome? Renewing your marriage vows can be a symbolic start. Reenergizing your attitude towards your companion will bring you closer to your objective.

You have to keep working at influencing the outcome by keeping your purpose alive and your desired outcome prominent in your mind.

Refreshing your living-on-purpose perspective often stems from a significant life-changing event. To rekindle this feeling, think of some of the many "firsts" in your life—your first job, first date, or first skydive. In each instance there was an initial period of hesitant uncertainty—perhaps even "butterflies" in your stomach—as you struggled with the discomfort of the unfamiliar. Gradually, as you gained more experience, hesitation was replaced with growing confidence. Just as success breeds greater confidence, overconfidence breeds humility. It is only when the rules are changed that you truly begin to understand what you were so positive that you already knew. Just ask any skilled golfer about the impact of the pro suggesting a change in grip or foot position. Some will fight it and forego improvement in favor of comfortable mediocrity; others will open-mindedly cherish the opportunity to become a beginner again—unsure, open to suggestion, and destined to improve.

When recreating this newness of being a beginner, one of your biggest challenges can be feeling less sure about everything. You will feel a sense of immediacy and of living in the moment. It can also lead to breakthrough levels of achievement. Whether it is your relationship with your spouse, your parents, or your clients, seeing your progress and your setbacks with a sense of newness and anticipation enables you to ask new questions and enjoy the thrill of accomplishing something for the first time— all over again—free of history, free of baggage. Specifically, you will escape from the limiting expectations of how things are supposed to be and how "this time" compares to the "last time we did this." You will be free to do things differently and to develop a new understanding as you share new experiences and you create a sense of rebirth in your relationship.

Think about an important relationship in your life that could use "rejuvenation." Take a moment to write down three ways you can "keep the spark alive" by returning to the way you felt at the beginning. Use Exercise 3 to list your thoughts, intentions, and activities.

Exercise 3: Keeping The Spark Alive

List three ways you can rekindle the newness to keep the spark alive in your relationship with _____
(name who or what).

1._____

2._____

3._____

Making progress requires that you keep the purpose, intent, and desired outcome foremost in your mind. Without these, any progress is purely accidental. Living becomes a series of unplanned yet interconnected events with unpredictable and inconsistent outcomes. By instilling the "Living on Purpose" perspective, your goal is the achievement of your desired outcome. It is the intended result of your action.

Stay young!

Stay new!

Stay alive!

Setting And Sharing Goals

Pick up any book on goal setting and you will see a statement such as the following: "Goals need to be clear, measurable, attainable, believable, and divisible into smaller steps on a timeline." A goal also needs to be written and reviewed regularly to:

★ Keep it vivid in your mind

★ Help you focus on the deliberate actions required to achieve it

★ Make sure the goal itself remains a high priority

★ Ensure your goal is truly yours, rather than only something others want you to do.

No matter how hard you try, you cannot set a goal for someone else. You can only create one for yourself. This is one of the secrets of great coaches—the skill to get their team to take personal ownership of a common, shared goal—individual commitment to a group effort. A dynamic synergy results when many minds work towards a common purpose. Better results...quicker results...better resource allocation...shared learning...shared ownership.

Sharing a *goal* with others gives you all a *common purpose*; sharing an *outcome* gives you a *common experience*. Take the example of a World Series champion baseball dynasty like the New York Yankees or a perennial World Cup champion soccer team such as Brazil. Winning the championship has two levels: the shared team victory and the personal pleasure experienced by each team member who contributed to that goal. Although the shared group outcome will diminish over time, individual team members will continue to savor their personal experience forever.

When your past successes are more important and dominate your present experiences, you reminisce. Remembering your glory days from high school, college, or military service is one thing. Continuing to relive them is another.

When you have big plans for future achievement, you strive.

Think of it as a continuum ranging from past focus to future focus.

There are many issues that surface with living in the past, so it is important to know your orientation. We often hear new parents proudly recount stories of their child's progress. But they do not live in the past of that child's achievement. Planning for their own and their children's future, regardless of age, gives these parents the motivation to meet the challenges of each day. Where do you fall on this continuum? Use the scale in Exercise 4 to mark the place where your balance lies.

Exercise 4: Are You Future-Oriented Or Past-Oriented?

What is your orientation—reminiscing about the past or striving towards the future?

Past Success _____Future Achievement

   -10   -5   0   +5   +10

 (Reminisce)   (Strive)

You may want to take corrective action to disentangle yourself from past memories so you can focus on creating an even more exciting future!

Achieving Goals In Your Mind

Goal achievement does not just happen; it is a process of continuously benchmarking your improvement and striving higher. It is a spiral type of process where you:

—assess your capabilities,

   o set a goal,

      ■ work at achieving the goal (practice),

         • realize that you can achieve it,

   o actually achieve it,

    ■ enjoy your success,

     • reassess your capabilities,

      o set a higher goal,

       ■ work at achieving the goal,

        • and so on...

Goal attainment occurs at two levels:

1. The objective level is the "black and white" of assessing your capabilities, perfecting skills, and achieving the goal

2. The subjective level of setting the goal, realizing your capability, enjoyment of the outcome, reassessing what to do next, and setting a more challenging target pulls you forward

Much of the subjective level involves visualizing the successful achievement of the goal.

Your ability to imagine is so strong that you can actually create the subjective feelings associated with enjoying the goal achievement's outcome long before the actual goal attainment. When you visualize, you are "tricking" yourself—but in a good way. You are imagining that you have achieved what you want *before* actually achieving it. Visualizing prepares you for the experience and puts you at ease. Visualizing your success is often recommended to anyone seeking to make a change—particularly job seekers, politicians, public speakers, sales executives, and athletes.

You can use visualization to achieve superior results. Psychologists classify the human mind as having conscious and unconscious (or subconscious) properties. The unconscious dimension of the mind does not distinguish between fact and fiction. So, if you use your powers of positive thinking and visualization to repeatedly (and intentionally) feed your mind information about a successful specific accomplishment, your unconscious mind will gradually believe that you have actually accomplished your goal.

When a belief is strong enough, your unconscious mind accepts the fiction of positive expectations as the real achievement of the goal's value. World-class athletes use this tactic. For example, Olympic-level high divers are trained to visualize the successful completion of every dive before making it. A diver will totally visualize her dive experience: the sounds, the smells, the feel of the breeze, each and every step she must complete. As she visualizes, her muscles twitch in response, as if actually performing the dive. Doing this helps calm jittery nerves and prepares her confidence to achieve the dive mechanics she wants. In her mind's eye, she has the perfect dive within her grasp; she already believes she has achieved her goal!

Beliefs Turn Into Paradigms

When you believe something *without question*, it becomes part of your personal belief—a *paradigm*.

A paradigm is a fundamental way of thinking that contains a set of assumptions on which you base your thoughts and actions. Describing something as a paradigm is not a value judgment; it is an acknowledgment of it as a belief that shapes your attitudes and actions. For example, Europeans once shared the centuries-long belief that Earth was the center of the universe. Historically, when church and state were virtually combined as one, to think otherwise was considered heresy, punishable by excommunication (as Galileo found out). Although incorrect, this strongly held belief was a paradigm that governed people's lives and clouded their judgment.

Similarly, the pre-suffrage attitude of men towards the ability of women to make "important" political decisions was a paradigm in its day. Obviously, not all paradigms are correct, but because they are strongly held, they are believed correct until proven wrong. Even then, many people continue to cling to them.

Belief in an afterlife or in reincarnation, belief in the efficiency of an assembly line, belief in the big-box store approach to retailing—these are all examples of paradigms held to be true by certain groups of people. Although you base your decisions on your individual set of beliefs, you share many of these beliefs with others in society. Because of these shared beliefs, you are able to communicate and cooperate with others and live in an orderly way.

Create Your Own Paradigm Shift

Do you believe your future will unfold according to a grand scheme controlled by influences outside of your control? Do you believe your future will be a variation on random events? Do you believe your past determines your future? Or, do you believe your future is yours to create—that it can be different from either your present or your past?

This is the paradigm that underlies this book:

THE LIVING ON PURPOSE PARADIGM

When you purposely set goals and achieve them,
you can create a future that can be
different from either your present or your past.
You can proactively pull yourself towards the future
you want!

What paradigm shifts do you want to create?

Your paradigms (your beliefs) stem from your values and they are reflected in your actions. Even maintaining your personal status quo requires effort. Simply doing nothing leads to change. How is that? With inertia, you will gain weight, lose muscle tone, and become less (or from a weight gain perspective, *more*) of what you were in the past.

* ★ Who are you?

* ★ Who do you want to become?

* ★ What have others successfully done in quest of this dream?

* ★ What new assets and resources do you need to attract into your life?

* ★ What are you willing to do about it?

* ★ What are you doing about it?

Those Who Have Shifted Paradigms

At the 1960 Olympics, Wilma Rudolph, a teenager born and raised in Tennessee, set the world on fire with her sprinting. Her story started with a great personal tragedy. She was the twentieth of twenty-two children born to a poor Tennessee railroad porter and his wife in the days of the segregated South. As a child, she had been diagnosed with poliomyelitis, a crippling disease that atrophies the muscles. At that time, polio had no known cure, prevention, or treatment. Wilma was told that she would never walk normally again. Running was out of the question. As a young girl, she needed heavy metal leg braces to assist her weakened leg muscles. Her family, however, was determined to help her live normally. Encouraged and assisted by her parents and siblings, she battled against the debilitating effects of polio and broke the polio paradigm. Not only was she rehabilitated, but she overcame the effects of the disease and won 1960 Olympic Gold medals—three times!

Lance Armstrong, cancer survivor and seven-time Tour de France cycling champion, also faced incredibly challenging circumstances. Already a world-class cyclist, Lance was stricken with multiple severe forms of cancers. Combining his own fierce determination with medical technology, he overcame brain cancer, lung cancer, and testicular cancer. Following surgery and rehabilitation in the mid-1990s, Lance returned to world-class competition, including winning the grueling Tour de France three-week-long bicycle endurance race every year from 1999 to 2005.

As a young adult, Canada's Terry Fox was diagnosed with bone cancer; his right leg was amputated above the knee. Determined to lead a life with purpose, Terry set his sights on raising money for cancer research by running across Canada. Starting with his artificial leg touching the Atlantic Ocean in St. Johns, Newfoundland, Terry set off for his hometown, Port Coquitlam, on the Pacific Coast. He ran 26 miles (over 41.8 kilometers) most days (the equivalent of an Olympic marathon) for 143 days and covered 3,339 miles (5,373 kilometers). This would be a wondrous feat for anyone—but to do it on one leg captured the imagination of millions of Canadians. Terry was not able to complete his run, but his spirit lives on through the annual Terry Fox Day, celebrated as a cancer awareness and fund-raising event across Canada. Even though Terry died in 1981, to date over $400 million has been raised worldwide for cancer research in his name.

Values and goals are the building blocks of your Living on Purpose Paradigm program. It is a focused, evolutionary, and disciplined pathway to *purposeful* change. It is like adopting a personal mantra similar to the U.S. Army's "Be all that you can be" slogan. By applying discipline, effort, and consistency at a fundamental level, you can shape a future different from your past. Although your values set the tone, your goals are the ends that bring you closer to reinforcing your values. The processes you apply to achieve these goals also support your values. For example, a value of good health has goals related to diet and exercise; a value of close personal relationships includes goals relating to honesty and spending more time with the ones you love. Choosing these goal paths leads to reinforcing these values.

By using your values to set your goals and then using your goals to develop your assets and to attract resources that strengthen and reinforce your values, you create a dynamic relationship that (1) strengthens your vision of your future and (2) pulls you in the direction of your choice—consistent with your beliefs and aligned with your paradigms.

Let's examine this more fully.

Integrating Values, Goals, And Assets

Your goals are the embodiment of your values. Goals imply processes or strategies for achieving them. Goal processes involve the tactics you implement to:

★ Influence the outcome of your actions

★ Attract the tools necessary to achieve your goals

★ Live according to your values

Assets can be internal or external. Internal assets are the result of your "you-ness"—the sum of the physical, intellectual, social, spiritual, and interactive you—that empowers you to live according to your values. External assets are the resources you attract into your life to help you achieve your goals. Your internal assets and external resources better position you to develop, reinforce, and expand upon your values in the future.

That is the theory, but how does it work in real life? Basically, we are describing a gradual progression from the theoretical abstract to the operable concrete. The following is an example of how this process could work—integrating both internal assets with external resources:

The adult population today is evolving from being baby boomer dominated to being under the control of the first cyber generation. Communication has moved from one-to-one conversations over the family telephone (seemingly one step up from smoke signals) to 24/7 instant text messaging within groups of likeminded individuals. The basic 1960–1990s backdrop of conspicuous consumption and potential nuclear holocaust has shifted to a 21ˢᵗ century backdrop of ever-accelerating technological innovation. Now, "we" (the baby boomers) have become the "they" who are handing the world over to our children. The 21ˢᵗ century paradigm is shifting towards issues that include global resource depletion: fresh water shortages, global warming, species extinction, and food supply depletion. Toxicity, trash, and pace of the global spread of disease continually increase. These catastrophic threats are the present day's boogey man. Given this backdrop, what are some of the constructive beliefs, values, and goals that a forward-looking individual might hold?

Note the positive nature of the statements in the following example:

Belief: I believe that part of our responsibility as members of the human family is to ensure that we protect the world that has been entrusted to our care, as best as our priorities and resources permit. More specifically, we should establish daily habits of conservation and recycling. My individual efforts can make a difference when compounded by others doing likewise.

Value: I place value in conservation and will patronize businesses that do likewise by reducing wasteful consumer packaging that has not been or cannot be recycled.

Asset (internal): I am a concerned citizen. I have developed habits that reduce public litter. I do not leave electrical lights on in unoccupied rooms and I recycle paper, cardboard, tin, and plastic. I turn down the thermostat in cold weather and wear a sweater, and turn up the thermostat in warm weather so that less energy is consumed.

Resource (external assets): I am a concerned recycler in a neighborhood of concerned recyclers.

Goal: In the next three years, I will become a model conservationist and recycler. Our neighborhood of model recyclers will be recognized for our example and our innovative actions.

Goal Achievement Process: I will spearhead forming a commit-tee to hold monthly neighborhood open forums at the local library where we can discuss and share conservation secrets, suc-cesses, and practices with like-minded neighbors. We will meet with local politicians to make sure that they share and espouse this priority.

In this way, the "value" and "belief" trigger the goal process and set the goal in motion. Using available resources, the goal process moves the asset's potential to a higher level. The value becomes more concrete. The belief is reinforced and the world is made a better place.

Now it is time to take a preliminary look at how your beliefs and values come together with your assets to form your own per-sonal reality. Start by articulating your beliefs and values within the context of a personal life statement. Let it tie your assets to your beliefs. See how you can shape your future goal and goal processes' direction.

Asserting Your Life Statement

You have completed the "goal brainstorming" from "Moving Forward" at the beginning of the book as well as the Mind-Stretcher exercises in Chapter 1. Now it is time for a greater challenge that will make you stretch even further....loosening up those rusty goal-setting muscles.

Get some paper and a pen. Suspend your judgment and pre-pare to integrate all of the information you have ever compiled in your life into this single life statement: *I can use my assets to shape the best life available—both now and in the future!*

Can you do this? Absolutely. The following nine steps will help you formulate how you can get there. Write down your answers as completely as possible.

1. Realistically describe the life that you have right now—how you are applying your assets at the moment.

2. Describe the best possible version of your current life, given the assets and resources you have now.

3. Identify the changes needed to make these two lists congruent. What changes must happen to transform your current life into your best possible life available right now and in the future?

4. Identify the priority and time frame required to complete each change.

5. Develop progress-tracking mechanisms for each change.

6. Identify how this present "best possible life" compares to the one you want to live at a specific future date (i.e., three years from now).

7. Identify the changes needed to achieve that future life on that schedule (per items 4 and 6).

8. Decide how committed you are to achieving these life changes and edit as necessary.

9. Just do it—do something that moves you closer to each of your goals each day.

If you truly want it, work towards it—every day.

Look into your future to see where this can lead. Let your vision of your best possible future help you focus on the actions that need to be taken and the time frame required, to move your current situation towards your best possible future situation.

By establishing your best possible current and future situations and the actions needed to achieve them, you are defining the goals required to bring your life into harmony with your expectations.

The best time to build your future life is now. Wishing and hoping for change will not make it happen. Living in the present—according to your future vision—will.

Leverage Assets To Achieve Goals

Once created, an asset can be leveraged to help achieve other goals. This is where your sense of living on purpose comes in. As your asset grows, your vision expands and greater goals can be set. When your goal is achieved and materializes as an enhancement to your assets, you can use it to work towards a larger goal. What is the result? A visionary dream of unstoppable dimension—perhaps (going back to the example above) even starting a foundation that monitors, measures, and disseminates new recycling and energy conservation strategies throughout the world. Depending upon where you live, in 2015, your efforts might be recognized with the Order of Canada, the U.S. Presidential Medal of Freedom, a British knighthood, or the newly created Nobel Prize for Ecology!

After identifying your impassioned interests, the first step is developing your talents (assets) into skills (higher level assets). On the theoretical side, the tight strategy-based interplay between values, goals, and assets is needed, with the asset becoming the tangible embodiment of both the value and the goal. On the operational side, the *Tactical Goal Achievement Process*—the "how-to" dimension—is where the visionary coaching, the perspective, the evaluative process, the recommended course of action, the implementation of change, and the feedback process of practicing for "perfection" are brought together in a structured package to continually raise the bar as the asset is perfected in quest of the goal.

The relationships between the value, the goal, and the asset are interactive ones. The goal focuses on the asset and then feeds upon the successful improvement in the asset, to create an even larger goal and an evolving goal achievement process.

The dynamic, interactive relationship among the Value, the Goal, and the Goal Achievement Process affects the potential of the assets and resources associated with it. But which goals? What assets? Each individual has many different interests in his or her life and many diverse goals such as achieving quarterly business sales objectives, losing 35 pounds of excess lovability (a.k.a. fat), or learning Spanish. Obviously, not all goals fit conveniently into one simple category. We need a method to organize and categorize our goals and assets according to our interests and capabilities. In the next chapter, we will explore how the Goal Achievement Process relates to the different categories of assets. There, we will introduce the Whole Person Concept as a means of gathering perspective on our different categories of assets, resources, and goals.

Chapter 3
The Whole Person Concept
And The Five Quotients

If someone were to ask you to describe yourself, you might use categories such as age, gender, marital status, occupation, education, and so on. Depending on your age, or major life events such as getting married or parenthood, how you might describe yourself will change. Obviously, you have a concept of who you are in relation to others. However, when scientists look at you, they tend to chop you up into different parts according to their specialties—sort of like looking at the individual trees and never realizing you are in the middle of a forest. This division is necessary for the development of scientific theory and for ranking you against an ideal or an average. But, once that has been done, putting you back together again is equally necessary.

Your values and your goals exist within you. These are special because of you. You have many dimensions and so do your goals. Even more potential goals are thrust at you every day. Watch television any morning and you will see a myriad of goals dangled in front of you in easy segments ranging from 30 seconds to 30 minutes: whiten your teeth overnight…change the color of your hair…stop smoking with this patch. But you are more than these snippets of pop culture. Yes, you have a body that needs to be taken care of, but you also have a mind, a family, friends, and a sense of spirituality. Every day you interact with others on many different levels.

The Whole Person Concept Provides
A Frame Of Reference

You have likely heard the old story of the five blindfolded sci-entists who encountered an elephant. One touched the ear, another the tail, another a tusk, another the leg, and the last encountered the trunk. Because their blindfolds limited their information and their sensory perceptions were different, they would not accept each other's description and they could not agree on what they were touching. Unlike these scientists, you have an all-encompassing perspective and a holistic understand-ing. Intuitively, you can link their observations together to visu-alize the elephant.

This same story has a real-life counterpart. As noted above, for years scientists have studied and measured different aspects of humanity such as intellect, physique, emotion, empathy, efficiency of the body's organs and systems. Like the blindfolded scientists who experienced the elephant for the first time, scientific special-izations have been limiting too. Modern scientists need a unify-ing perspective to create a holistic understanding. This frame of reference has been named the "Whole Person Concept." It is a well-rounded perspective representing the most significant aspects of your individuality—particularly your mental intelli-gence, physical body, sense of spirituality, and emotional responses in social situations.

Let's confirm what assets and resources you have at your dis-posal. Remember, your assets are the inner capabilities that you bring; your resources are the external things you attract into your life.

Your assets include:

★ Your personal strengths and interests (intellectual)

★ Your physical health (physical)

★ Your education and knowledge (intellectual)

★ Your business acumen (intellectual)

★ Your life experiences that you use to help make decisions (intellectual)

★ Your quest for meaning in life (spiritual)

★ Your sense of religion (spiritual)

Your resources include:

★ Your family and work relationships (social)

★ Your personality and how you deal with stress (social)

★ Your monetary and investment wealth (financial)

★ Your social and societal relationships (social)

★ People from whom you seek advice (social)

Obviously, this summary is representative rather than all-inclusive. Your assets and resources are the summation of not only what you are, but also of what you value, what you have accumulated, and what you have retained from your past. How you utilize this information forms the stepping-stones to your future.

Integrating Assets And Resources

The Whole Person Concept, then, starts with individual measurements of intellect, emotional stability, physical fitness, and spirituality and overlays them to develop a representation of the individual. Scientists have established quotients measuring the capability and potential of these attributes. Their individual measurements (scores) are compared on scales relative to ideals such as the commonly known Intelligence Quotient or IQ. Here the top 2% of population have IQ scores over 148 and are eligible for MENSA membership. On a physical fitness level, the top 2% would be the ones you see on TV in the Hawaiian Ironman Endurance Championship where competitors swim 2.4 miles, cycle 112 miles, and then run a 26.2 mile marathon. The best male competitors complete this in under 8½ hours. Personally, I get tired just thinking about it!

Traditional views of the Whole Person Concept deal with intellectual, physical, social/emotional, and spiritual dimensions, and tend to look at the individual as an isolated being. The Traditional Whole Person Concept (Diagram 1) integrates these four asset areas:

1. Mental capability (Intelligence Quotient)

2. Body function (Physical Quotient)

3. Social interaction (Emotional Quotient)

4. Spirituality (Spiritual Quotient)

Diagram 1: Traditional Whole Person Concept

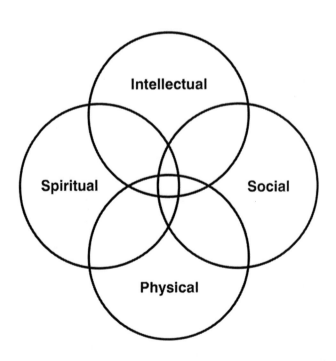

Although a great starting point, this four-sector view addresses only your internal assets. It excludes your give-and-take interaction with factors outside of your body and mind (people, places, things). A fifth category needs to be integrated into the Whole Person Concept (Diagram 2) to represent this interactive dimension. I call it the "Financial Quotient." It focuses on how you understand your strengths and weaknesses in the other four categories, *plus* how you use your skills to establish an exchange value when you interact with other people.

Our Expanded Whole Person Concept (Diagram 2) integrates these five asset areas:

1. Mental capability (Intelligence Quotient)

2. Body function (Physical Quotient)

3. Social interaction (Emotional Quotient)

4. Spirituality (Spiritual Quotient)

5. Interactive exchange value (Financial Quotient)

Diagram 2: Expanded Whole Person Concept

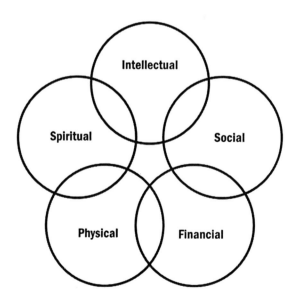

Through this five-factor Whole Person Concept, you will see yourself not as an isolated individual, but as a dynamic person actively involved in give-and-take with others as you apply your assets and resources to give life to your dreams. Let's examine the Financial Quotient in more detail.

The Financial Quotient

You constantly interact on many different levels—giving, taking, sharing, creating, and exchanging value with others. Progress occurs and worth is realized at this interactive level. Your Financial Quotient integrates your personal "economic" orientation with the other aspects of the Whole Person Concept. To determine your own interactive values, answer the following questions:

★ How do you establish your personal worth, relative to others?

★ How do you decide how much something you do is worth to yourself and to others?

★ How do you add value or enhance the value you offer to others?

★ Do you decide this amount yourself, or do you let others decide?

★ How do you learn to become financially smart?

Whoa—wait a minute! Personal values, assessing value, adding value, creating value—this is getting confusing! Are terms and definitions being mixed here? No, not really. Some are subjective and some objective. Subjectively, your "personal values" are those concepts in which you place greatest worth. Objectively, the work you do creates value for which you are compensated and is based on the merit that others place in your work.

Your Financial Quotient represents more than just money.

Much of your Financial Quotient was nurtured within you by your parents through their example of where they placed value and how they dealt with money and relationships. Part comes from your family dynamics and part from schoolroom learning. Part comes from your sense of self-esteem. You use your Intellectual, Spiritual, Physical, and Emotional Quotients to develop your sense of values in all types of interpersonal exchanges, particularly where an asset's worth is enhanced (i.e., value added).

Your Financial Quotient comes into play whenever there is an exchange of items. It helps determine how you establish the value of one item compared to the worth of another, whether you are engaged in a barter system, a negotiation, an auction, or retail. Your Financial Quotient also affects how you value your personal effort, your accumulated wealth, and your potential to create new wealth. Additionally, it is used to validate the roles of the individuals involved in a relationship.

The Financial Quotient focuses on the value creation/exchange dimension. As the seed of your "money smarts," it adds the objective, interactive level to the subjective, personal side of the Whole Person Concept, so that it applies to everyday interactions. Your Financial Quotient is a key differentiating skill set. It determines not only your level of wealth, but more importantly your ability to convert the wealth that you have into meaningful enjoyment of all of your other assets.

Sometimes your Physical Quotient reacts to money. Imagine winning the lottery or losing your job. The sudden gain or loss of money or economic value can cause physiological changes ranging from "off-the-wall" excitement to cold sweats to fainting or even heart attacks. It emphasizes the way you relate to money and other aspects of economic value creation. It is about wealth creation and wealth preservation, loss recovery, and debt management. Your Financial Quotient establishes your ability to gather, grow, conserve, and transfer your wealth and your attitudes about wealth to your children, and in many instances how you go about these activities too.

Although other quotients come into play, your Financial Quotient sets the tone. This concept is based on social exchange theory and reciprocity theory, branches of sociology and social psychology. Social exchange theory states that, while all relationships have give-and-take, the balance of this exchange is not always equal. Rather, relationships are affected by factors such as:

★ Each party's concept of fairness

★ What assets you put value in, along with the how and why

★ The interplay between what you put into a relationship and what you get out of it

★ The quality of relationships you believe you deserve

The give-and-take of establishing relative worth takes in a multitude of variables and leads to either an abundance or a scarcity mentality (i.e., the glass is half full or half empty).

Including the Financial Quotient in the Whole Person Concept adds a dimension of economic and social interaction. It takes the Whole Person Concept from a focus on the "inner" assets of intellect, physical well-being, spirituality, and emotions, and adds the "external" resources of the interactive dimension. I see each of these five quotients of the Whole Person Concept as equally important to your goals and goal achievement.

Your Attitude Towards Money

Do you believe money is plentiful or scarce? Abundance thinking versus scarcity thinking is demonstrated in how you relate to others in a commercial environment. It also determines your ability to make long-term decisions and commitments.

How so? In many instances, long-term commitment requires financial staying power. Consider the concept of "quantity versus quality." Do you prefer low-priced, low-quality goods over high-priced, high-quality goods? Or do you believe in the old adage about wanting your cake and eating it too? Is this why you wait for the "good stuff" to go on sale before you buy it? Do you need the latest model car, or would you rather get one more year out of a car that has been paid off and works perfectly well? At the time of this writing, gasoline prices in North America had risen to over $4.00 U.S. per gallon ($1.37 Cdn. per liter. There are 3.8 liters in a gallon, so that's $5.21 a gallon in Canada.). European gasoline prices were even higher, exceeding $8.00 U.S. per gallon. People are concerned about both the long-term future availability of gasoline and the rise in price. Ethanol is being legislated as an additive to stretch out the gasoline supply. While future prices may fluctuate, how individuals respond to the long-term trend should remain consistent. Future car replacement decisions, no doubt, will be affected by this higher operating cost, yet few individuals are rushing to replace their relatively new, expensive, low-efficiency vehicles with equally or more expensive new, high-efficiency, "green" vehicles. (Obviously, other reasons—i.e., Financial—that have nothing to do with Intellectual, Physical, Spiritual, or Emotional Quotients can affect their decision making.)

Your Financial Quotient shows up in your attitudes and actions towards risk, debt, and recurring expenses. It also factors into interpersonal relationships—especially when two people who share financial resources have different sets of values and goals. You probably know many couples in which one is a spender and the other is a saver. This combination often produces the "irreconcilable differences" that fill many divorce courts. When you get two spenders together, the result can be the same, but the focus might shift to the bankruptcy courts. Either way, it all comes back to your Financial Quotient.

Typically, you will discover you have one quotient of the Whole Person Concept that dominates. Usually it is not the financial that dominates, but it is reflected in your priorities regarding your family, your charitable works, your continuing education, or your need for physical comforts. This is your comfort zone, where you routinely focus. However, to build balance in the lifestyle you want, you need to integrate all five dimensions. The Whole Person Concept framework ties it all together. What follows is example of the integrated Whole Person Concept.

How A Golfer Selects A Golf Course

This example demonstrates how a golfer might use the Whole Person Concept to make a decision about where to play.

When we compare the golfing enthusiast to the average golfer, along with cost, factors such as pace of play, quality of greens and fairways, the types and quality of services ranging from valet parking to the pro shop and locker rooms, and 19th-hole camaraderie and social status all come into consideration.

Course A: This course is open to the public. Anyone can play on a first-come, first-served basis. You pay for the services you use and take away whatever you brought with you (except for lost golf balls). You are free to enjoy the course equally with all the other golfers who choose to play on any given day regardless of your skill level, or the skill levels of the foursomes in front and behind you. Green fees are $75.00 per round per player, $50.00 after 2:00 PM. Carts are available at an additional fee. To be profitable, the club needs to have a foursome approaching each tee as the previous foursome reaches the green. For 18 holes, this equates to approximately 144 players on the course. If there are several par-five holes, you can add another foursome halfway up each fairway. Having four par-five holes means accommodating 16 more players, bringing the total to 160 players for the owner's ideal optimum loading. Of course, optimum loading means that you need to watch for the occasional golf ball whizzing over your head and wait around for the foursome ahead of you to get out of range. If there are a lot of social golfers and duffers, your score may be an unenjoyable 10 strokes higher because you were "off your game." Parking, restaurant and bar, pro shop, changing rooms, etc., are considered either profit centers or necessary expenses.

Course B: This private club has initiation fees of $75,000 and annual dues of $10,000, a minimum bar/dining tab of $500 per month, and a strict dress code. Given the fee structure, Club B does not require the same optimum loading as Course A does to break even and members would revolt if it achieved that same level of course loading. Although your game would be unhurried, you would spend less time here than on Course A because you do not have to wait between holes. Your score will be consistent because the overall experience is more consistent than on Course A. From valet parking to relaxing with several friends at the 19th hole, there will be a noticeable difference in your experience.

Will there be a difference in the enjoyment of a round on Course A versus Course B? Will the average caliber of play be the same on both courses? Will one course likely have more doctors, lawyers, executives, and business owners as players than the other? Will the makes and models of cars parked be the same in both course parking lots? Will the same people come back to play week after week at both courses? Will there be a group of people who choose Club B over Club A solely because of the exclusive nature of its membership?

Yes, there is a social element. Yes, there may be an intellectual element. There is definitely a physical element. For some, there is even a spiritual element. In spite of these factors, the overriding element in the choice of whether to play at Course A or Course B usually comes down to the financial element. I say "usually" because there will always be those individuals who will sacrifice in other areas of their life in order to enjoy the status of exclusive private club membership—just as there are those who insist that their child be educated at a particular private school.

In summary, by introducing the Whole Person Concept, we have subclassified assets, resources, goals, and values in five categories: physical, spiritual, social, intellectual, and financial. We have done this so you can better allocate your assets to these sectors. This is for convenience and ease of understanding only. Ultimately, the real value remains in the synergy created through their integration into you as a " whole person." A quick Internet search reveals that that the gifts in the song "The 12 Days of Christmas" are valued at over $78,000—while at the same time, chemically, your body is worth the princely sum of approximately $4.50 (about the same as a gallon or two of gasoline!). But remember, when it comes to "you" and the true value of your "you-ness," the whole will always be much greater than the sum of the parts!

Chapter 4
A New Shift In Thinking

Imagine shaking off the shackles of years of couch potato-dom. Consider throwing your old self into the recycling bin for lipid lovers! With a new zest for life you say, "I'm going to join a gym and get fit!" There you are at the glass door, looking inside at the warm, lithe bodies beckoning you to a healthier world....

It's the first time you've entered a gym. You hesitate, just inside the door, feeling a little awkward and out of place. Looking around, you see all kinds of weird contraptions. You might recognize the treadmills and stationary bikes, but the rest look like medieval instruments of torture. You're not sure about this, but you're determined to go ahead with your health improvement goal. A nice young woman takes you around and gives you an overview of each instrument of torture (oops, I mean "muscle building machine"). She measures your height, weight, body mass (BMI), and blood pressure. She records your dietary likes and dislikes. She might have some charts ready to show you how you stack up compared to an Olympic decathlon gold medalist. Then, batting her eyes and smiling sweetly, she asks you what your goals are. You stammer something in reply...then the dream ends as you meet your new coach, Chip, lovingly known as "the trainer from hell." Why "Chip?" Well, his dad's name is "Rocky."

Chip lays out your fitness program and your schedule. He shows you how to properly use each apparatus. There are aerobic machines like the stationary bike and treadmill for building stamina and weight loss, anaerobic machines with all kinds of springs and weights and pulleys for building muscle mass. You start your new "high protein-low carb" diet program designed to cleanse your innards and to make sure that only good stuff goes in your mouth. After all, "garbage in equals garbage out!"

Now fast-forward eight weeks. You're greeted by first name as you enter the gym. Your weight and BMI are down a lot. You're comfortable with all the different machines and what they are for. You know your routines and Chip isn't so bad once you get to know him. You have your three-month progress targets and actual performance to date charted out and you're on track. You know that at Week 13 you'll have a reassessment and there may be some tweaking based upon how well you've progressed. Everything's going swell! You're glad that you started your health improvement goal and wonder why you didn't do it years ago.

As you drive home from the gym, you're pleased with your success in getting into the fitness habit. Your mind drifts and you find yourself thinking about your life. You wonder why you can't apply this same approach to other areas in your life.

Well, you can! Let's look at the four elements that you have put in place by establishing your fitness goal:

1. **Element One:** *Taking Stock*—**The Value/Asset Inventory.** You assessed your current status (weight, height, BMI, etc.) and compared it to a standard model. This establishes your current status (what you already have—your assets and resources).

2. **Element Two:** *Focus*—**The Strategic Goal-Setting Level.** Based on your awareness of your resources and your preconceived values, you decided what you wanted to do. You built a strategic understanding of the relationships between your values and your assets/resources and what you want to do with them (your goal).

3. **Element Three:** *Empowerment*—**The Tactical Goal Achievement Process Level.** Based on the tools at hand, a goal achievement program was developed and you

implemented the specific tactical process required to enhance your capabilities and to achieve your goals.

4. **Element Four: *Persistence*—Keep the Goal Foremost in Mind.** This is your routine, your habits that keep pulling you back on target to make progress on your top priority goal.

You had progress charts to tell where you were relative to your goal and you have strategies to return you to your top priorities and your next steps. You also have Chip, your coach, helping you keep your big-picture goal in your mind. There is measurement, tracking, and accountability here that will be part of your Week 13 reassessment—and you are persistently working towards that deadline. Little children are experts at persistence. When a child has her mind set on something, she seldom hears the word *no*. In your goal-achieving activities you need to develop that same stick-to-it-ive-ness that you had as a child. When the grown-up in you says "no," let your inner child come forward to re-emphasize how important your goal is to your future enjoyment.

In a way, each quotient of our Whole Person Concept is an ideal, or theoretical construct. As you progress through this book, you will develop goals that apply to each of these areas. When you compare your own personal reality to your ideal, there will always be differences. These differences are very important because these go into your Goal Incubation Process. When you know what makes you feel most alive and consequently what creates the greatest satisfaction in your life, you will want more.

★ You will want to optimize your enjoyment of your assets.

★ You will identify what you need to attract into your life.

★ You will decide to take action.

★ You will become aware of how this gives your life purpose.

★ You will be acting on purpose.

A new goal is born! The seed of a goal achievement plan forms. To germinate that seed and activate your plan, you need a process that assesses the importance of these differences and develops a game plan to monitor your progress and modify your actions. When you apply this approach, your Goal Achievement Process becomes practical and achievable—capable of being implemented in the real world of your day-to-day life.

∞

This completes Part One. You have identified your greatest passions and you are ready to move on!

We have examined the need to categorize and focus on what you want to achieve. We have highlighted some of your passions in life. We have introduced the interplay between the goals that you set and the assets and resources that you use to achieve those goals. We introduced the five categories of the Whole Person Concept. Specifically, we have focused on five key goal and asset categories—intellectual, physical, social, spiritual, and financial. Your assets and resources fall within these categories. The goals you set are structured around how you want to utilize and enhance your assets and resources to live according to your values. We have introduced a four-stage process for goal achievement that includes (a) taking inventory, (b) focusing on what you want, (c) empowering your plan, and (d) through persistence, keep it "top of mind" memorable.

Part Two concentrates on the first two elements: Taking Stock—The Value/Asset Inventory and Focus—The Strategic Goal-Setting Level. Parts Three, Four, and Five address the other two elements: Empowerment—The Tactical Goal Achievement Process Level and Persistence—Keeping the Goal Foremost in Mind.

Moving on to Part Two now, you will discover the tools that sharpen your focus to achieve your goals effectively and efficiently. We will look at the importance of your strategic orientation to your assets and the tactical use of your assets to achieve your goals. By the end of Part Two, you will be much more comfortable with the five Whole Person categories and you will have established your top three priorities for each of them.

PART TWO

Activating Your "Whole Person"

FOCUS

First, have a definite, clear practical ideal; a goal, an objective....

Chapter 5
The Goal Achievement Process
Overview-Assets, Strategies, And Tactics

How do you choose a goal to work on? What is your starting point? From our perspective, you decide on a goal when you look at your assets and resources and say to yourself that there is something about them that rouses your passion or your curiosity, that gives you a sense of satisfaction (i.e., makes you feel alive), and you say to yourself, "I want more of this." For whatever reason, from this point, you start to work on defining and attaining a goal. First the asset (personal capability), then the desire (personal passion), then the goal (personal commitment).

What happens if you want to do something but still need to learn about it—or do not have the talent but still want to pursue something? Isn't that okay…like someone who dabbles in painting and has passion for it, but isn't any good at it? There are times when passion can get ahead of capability. We all know budding artists and enthusiastic bathtub Pavarotti-wannabes. These wonderful people exhibit strong passions in line with their goal. But what is their goal? It could be simply to immerse themselves in it and enjoy the visceral pleasure of "doing"; perhaps some day their enthusiasm may even lead them to advancing the art form. American folk artist Grandma Moses probably never thought that her paintings would someday sell for hundreds of thousands of dollars and grace the walls of the White House along with the Cézannes and Monets—come to think of it, Cézanne and Monet probably did not think about it either! What is important is that your goal is yours and not someone else's. Other people will always be willing to evaluate your performance. But as they do not know what your personal goal is, what difference does their opinion make? They may have an opinion of your work versus some ideal, but your personal best should always be more important to you than someone else's opinion.

Often you are told that your goals are your ends, that once a goal is set, you must move heaven and earth in your never-ending struggle to achieve that goal. Once you do, what next? You are back at square one, setting another goal.

Rather than this "make-it-or-break-it" approach, I see each goal as a stepping-stone that leads towards an even greater goal. No one goal is ever the be-all and end-all. It is always an opportunity to move through a doorway into a new dimension and towards a new set of opportunities and goals. Look at your goals as progressive steps that take you forward, on schedule, through your life's journey as you create the future you choose. Goals take on a new meaning when you adopt this perspective, and they can be divided into their strategic and tactical components.

Strategies And Tactics

The strategic level is where you set your big-picture "this is what I want to accomplish and why" vision. The tactical level is the "this is how I'm going to do it and when" implementation dimension.

The strategic component will be more visionary and will grow from your awareness of one of your assets to the point that you want to develop it in some manner. You know that activities related to this asset excite you, fire up your passions, and make you feel more alive—and you want more of it. You begin at a big-picture level to view your assets and resources as part of a progressive four-stage continuum. We call this strategic level The Goals Incubator. Its four stages are:

★ **Gather:** You can increase your supply by gathering more (i.e., quantity).

★ **Grow:** You can enhance your assets by improving the quality or having it grow organically (i.e., quality).

★ **Conserve:** You can conserve your assets or ration it out so that it lasts longer.

★ **Transfer/Eliminate:** You can give or share your assets with others, or just get rid of them.

Your choice among these four categories establishes your attitude and your highest intention for your asset/resource. Once you have decided on the strategic importance of the asset, you are ready to put your plan into action—to set your goal and to develop the tactics that will take you towards your bigger future.

Tactically, you always start with what you know and what you have. Whatever your goal is, it will require that you achieve a change in your asset. You need to identify the change required to achieve your goal and then to set about making it happen. Periodically, you need to evaluate your progress, reassess your goal, and take corrective action. There is a six-step process that I recommend you follow as your goal-achieving process. I call this the Tactical Goal Achievement Process:

1. **Define:** Set the goal with clarity.

2. **Collect Data:** Take inventory of your assets relative to the goal.

3. **Assess:** Evaluate your assets against the goal and identify missing elements.

4. **Plan/Recommend:** Establish and document how the change that you want will be achieved.

5. **Implement:** Work on achieving the change.

6. **Review:** Periodically review your progress and go back to Step 1.

You should consistently apply this six-step process to every goal.

These two perspectives, Strategic and Tactical, are fundamental to your success in any activity that you undertake on purpose. The Strategic Goals Incubator is the focus of Chapter 6, in which you will look at how you develop a goal. It examines your Asset Awareness and Strategic Goal Setting dimension much as you might look at hatching eggs as a chicken farmer. In Chapter 7 you will use the six-step Tactical Goal Achievement Process to develop your key priorities in each of the five Whole Person Concept categories.

Chapter 6
Your Goals Incubator—
The Quality Of Life Continuum

If goals were like chickens, you could get a bunch of goal eggs, place them under a light bulb to keep them warm, and eventually most of them would hatch into cute little yellow balls of feathers looking for goal nourishment. You could buy or build your own incubator with reasonable success. Temperature control, humidity control, and sanitation would take a bit of effort. You would have to remember to turn the eggs several times a day. But the main things needed would be patience and consistency, because each egg would take 3½ to 4 weeks to hatch. Chicks hatch ready to go. Goals do not.

Goals are not so easy to incubate and they must be carefully nurtured. Some do not get turned over enough and come out half-baked. Others hatch prematurely and do not have a chance. Some goals just stink and should never have been pursued in the first place. To successfully incubate a goal takes a great deal of care because not only is the idea important, but its nurturing also includes developing the process and allocating the resources that lead to its successful completion. You can incubate hundreds of chicken eggs at a time; however, in the developmental stages, each goal needs your undivided attention. You need to nourish your fledgling goals with well thought out strategies and appropriate tactics.

Strategies and tactics are two sides of the same coin. Through the strategic side, we create the big-picture view of what we want to accomplish. Your strategic intent is your long-term view. Typically, it will change slowly. In the course of putting your strategy into motion, you will have different goals related to it and at times you will employ different tactics as suits your needs.

Strategy is like the dial on an automatic washing machine, slowly moving from one stage of the cycle to the next in a predictable sequence. As mentioned in Chapter 5, your strategies form that four-stage Goals Incubator's continuum of Gather–Grow–Conserve–Transfer. That is, you stockpile an asset (Gather), allow it to compound on its own momentum or through your own tactical intervention (Grow), stretch the supply and availability of the asset (Conserve), or give up all or part of the asset to someone else (Transfer). Diagram 3 will help you visualize how the Goals Incubator is structured.

Diagram 3: The Goals Incubator

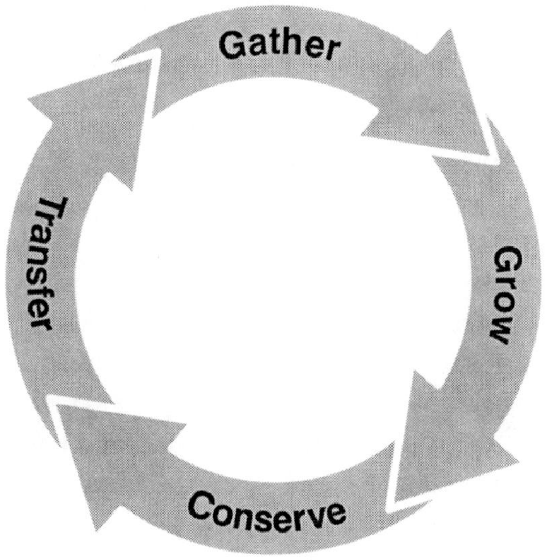

Conversely, the tactical side of the coin is the Goal Achievement Process. It supplies the techniques that you use to move towards achieving your goals. The Tactical Goal Achievement Process is the consistent approach that you employ to power, monitor, and measure your goal achievement progress. (More about this in Chapter 7.)

When you consider a category of your Whole Person Concept, such as your physical assets, you have a "strategic perception" of the worth of those assets—how you view your assets/resources and what you want to do with them. "What you want to do with them" becomes the seed of your incubating goal. This creates a context for your ideas and places them on a continuum of values. As an example, wanting to increase your stamina means something very different than wanting to lose weight. These are different strategic prescriptions that will lead to different tactical processes.

The longer a Goal Incubation "quality of life" cycle takes, the harder it is to observe. Think about the changes of the seasons. You have experienced this every year of your life and you know it is predictable. On the other hand, while you progressively grow older, you only experience aging once; nonetheless, you can see it all around you and can infer that all people age and that you will too. You understand the process of aging because you have seen it in other people. You understand that there is a predictable sequence of birth, development, degeneration, and decay. On an individual level, you understand that this as a linear process in which you personally go through the cycle only once—but even that might change. People now are living longer. Dipping into my financial planner background…20 years ago we would have projected life expectancy at being 70–75; now planners use 90–95 as life expectancy targets. From the larger point of view of a family or a society, it is cyclical and renewing. From the individual's point of view, this means that building wealth during the Gather and Grow stages is very critical because it must finance the Conserve stage, which may last as much as 30–40 years, far longer than previously expected.

Individually, you create your own cycle. You develop your interests and values based upon your assets and your resources. Your values and your assessment of your assets/resources stimulate your imagination to set the goals that shape your future. Regardless of its importance, unless a skill area excites you, you will not develop your assets related to it. You will let them languish while you focus on other areas that capture more of your imagination. You set goals. You take actions that move you towards the successful achievement of your goals. You accomplish results and accumulate possessions that are important to you. You eliminate things that you no longer need or want. In doing all this, you are going through the four stages of the Goals Incubator cycle: gathering, growing, conserving, and transferring/eliminating. ("Eliminating" is just another dimension of "transferring," where you no longer place any importance in the asset and do not care what happens to it.)

The Goals Incubator establishes the strategic importance that you place in each asset/resource within the five Whole Person Concept's dimensions. Ultimately, it helps you answer questions such as the following: Why is physical health important? What are your expectations of physical health at your current age? What are your lifestyle expectations in retirement and how will you finance them? What are your career aspirations for your children and how will you help finance them? The answers to these questions are personalized and based upon your values and your life priorities.

The Goals Incubator is sensitive to quality of life as an ideal that is easily taken for granted. The old adage "you don't know what you've got 'til it's gone" sums up this phenomenon. Everyone has an opinion of what quality of life means and what is needed to achieve or enhance it. For instance, as a child, you grow up in your parents' or guardians' home. When you move out on your own as a young adult, you may take many of their values with you. You expect you will have the same lifestyle to which you are accustomed. The quantity and quality of assets/resources that you took for granted as a child become necessities as you establish your independence. Your parents' home environment created an ideal, a comfort zone of expectation and lifestyle that you may try to recreate. However, you can become frustrated when you first try to attain the same quality of life. Gradually, you realize that the quality of life your parents have achieved did not occur overnight. Rather, it was based on their assets, and it evolved over a lifetime of working and saving (gathering), selecting, and developing (growing) their values and goals.

As a young adult, you transitioned towards independence, discovering that quality of life does not just happen—house, cars, computers, children, and physical well-being all take effort and have costs. Unrealistic expectations may have crept in and created overspending patterns (and debt) as you strove to achieve your ideal. Gradually, you learned that the quality of your living depends on not only your ability to gather, but also to grow, conserve, and transfer your assets and resources.

So is there a simple way to evaluate your assets? You started at the beginning of this book by looking at what makes you feel alive. You need to revisit this idea. At this point, it is more important to understand yourself than to define your specific asset. Look at the transition points. As you shift within the Goals Incubator cycle from "gather" to "grow" and from "grow" to "conserve," you may take quality of life for granted. The question is, "How do you move, delay moving, or realize that you must move from one stage to the next? Is it only when you get a surprise wake-up call that you realize things are changing or must change—that you need to take corrective action?" This is key. There are times when the transition from one stage to another is planned and pleasing—such as graduation or marriage—and there are other times when it is something that you want to delay or even avoid—such as marital breakdown or a heart attack. Thinking of the turning point that transitions you from one quality of life stage to another as a threshold—a threshold that you can take proactive action to bring on or to delay—means that, through your actions, you can influence the timing of the transition. You can proactively change your ways so that you do not always need to cross to the next stage before you are ready. I have developed Exercise 5 to kick-start your thinking about this.

For each Whole Person category, answer two questions. For the first question you select an asset and define why this type of asset is important to you. The second, which I call the "Wake-Up Call," is your "What the heck!*?&@!*" question. It identifies your "before it's too late" surprise. It makes you suddenly realize that things have changed—it is your "What would make you get you off your butt and do something about it?" answer. If it is not too late, it will serve as the motivator that spells the difference between your doctor telling you that unless you change your diet and lifestyle you are going to be a prime candidate for a heart attack and you actually having one. It is said there are three types of people: those who make things happen; those who watch things happen; and those who ask "What happened?" When your Wake-Up Call response requires immediate action, it will catapult you from being a potential watcher or a wonderer towards becoming the doer.

Exercise 5: Your "Why?" And Wake-Up Call Answers

Whole Person Concept Question	"Why This Is Important To You" Answer	The Wake-Up Call Answer: What major change would make you take action before it is too late?
Physical health example (i.e., freedom from aches and pains)	*My physical health allows me to enjoy the good things in life.*	*An emergency ambulance ride to the hospital because the doctor was right in telling me I was a prime candidate for a heart attack in the next 2 years because I'm an overweight couch potato.*
Why is my *physical* health important to me?		
Why is my *intellectual* health important to me?		
Why is my *social* health important to me?		
Why is my *spiritual* health important to me?		
Why is my *financial* health important to me?		

Your Wake-Up Call answer reveals an action or event that would tip the scale and upset your position relative to the value you set as your "Why" answer. This change affects your assets and resources. It is a change so significant in your strategic perception that it will crystallize your goal and set you in motion. Your objective here is to become sensitized to these Wake-Up Call answers and to move you closer to your present situation and to move you further from an irreversible point of no return. Look back at your answers. How can you prevent an irreversible physical, financial, spiritual, mental, or relationship breakdown? How can you make them more immediate? How can you move your need for change closer to your present reality? *Set Your Goals! Achieve Your Goals!*

Depending on your point of view, change can be positive or negative. Given the pace of most people's lives, it is easy to fall into passive, reactive patterns and even to assume an entitlement posture. By "entitlement," I mean assuming that others owe you something just for showing up. No effort is required on your part; you are "entitled" to be a passive benefactor. When this happens, any change becomes an ordeal and you often put off taking action until it is too late. On the other hand, when you take the pulse of what is important in your life, you are examining your goals. You are better equipped to take the proactive steps necessary to get off the self-entitlement couch and to proactively achieve whatever is most important to you. This will help you head off potential goals crises ranging from business failure or physical health issues to relationship, financial, or mental/emotional breakdown.

Assets/resources and your strategic perception of them reflect different stages in your personal growth and maturation. These in turn affect how you regard the quality of your life and how you treat your assets/resources, including whether you want to treasure them or give them away.

Your Strategic Perception Becomes
Your Strategic Positioning

Changes in attitude and awareness can happen gradually or suddenly. You place value in your assets/resources differently depending on what is going on in your life. These changes strategically position you within one of the four stages of the Goals Incubator and affect your thinking and actions. Typically, these four life stages correspond to the Gather–Grow–Conserve –Transfer continuum of Chapter 5. Recapping these stages from earlier:

* **Gather:** This is the initial stage. At this stage of life, you want to gather (or accumulate) a particular type of asset/resource from external sources.

* **Grow:** You seek to grow your own assets. At this second stage, you will use your assets more effectively and want them to compound on their own.

*
  Conserve: Here, you see your assets and resources begin to dwindle in quantity as they are consumed. You will want to conserve the remainder of your assets for future use.

* **Transfer:** Finally, you will outgrow your need for a resource or asset and you will want to transfer some or all of it to someone else. (Transfer also includes eliminate, which can be the same as transferring something into a black hole.)

These stages of the Goals Incubator need not occur in all assets, in the same manner, at the same time. They can overlap and they apply to various assets at the same or different times.

See how this applies to you. Look at your individual circumstances; refer back to Exercises 1 and 2, the Mind-Stretcher Questions, from Chapter 1. Use your answers to assess the quality of your life and see how it relates to your circumstances three years ago and to your desired situation three years from now. This establishes your strategic position (what you want to create) and your strategic focus (whether you need to gather, grow, conserve, or transfer assets).

As we move forward, keep the following questions in mind:

★ What are your assets?

★ What are your values? Interests? Passions?

★ What goals are you working towards?

★ What are the relationships between your values and goals?

★ How do these values and goals connect into your assets—your acquired "wealth" and resources?

★ Is there a process that you've been using (either consciously or unconsciously) to gather your wealth and augment your asset base?

★ How does this process use your assets to achieve your goals?

★ How will achieving this goal enhance your assets?

The Values/Assets Strategic Matrix

So you now have the Goals Incubator with its four strategic value positions—Gather, Grow, Conserve, and Transfer—plus you understand that these interact with the five basic Whole Person Concept asset categories. This equips you with the knowledge and tools to look at the passions in your life from a whole new perspective. Here is a summary of how these categories interact to create synergies. Notice that the first column includes both the Whole Person Concept category and an example of an asset. The other four columns connect the asset to the Goals Incubator's four stages. See how the different asset types can be gathered, grown, conserved, and transferred.

Table 2: Example Of A Value/Assets Matrix

Whole Person Category	Strategic Value Position			
Value/ Asset	Gather	Grow	Conserve	Transfer
Financial Health/ Retirement savings	Live within means, Save Education (control debt)	Investments and inflation Compounding	Risk management Taxation Good advice	Estate planning Insurance Philanthropy
Physical Health/ Age, weight, fitness, blood pressure	Balanced diet Re-energize (rest)	Hygiene Exercise	Eliminate toxins Flexibility	Role model Lifestyle habits Metabolic balance
Spiritual Health/ Peace of mind, religion, personal philosophy	Reading, talking, listening, praying	Charitable acts Ethical and moral behavior	Meditate Associate with like-minded people Be inspired to live your faith or to have faith in your life	Teach your children about responsibility, right and wrong
Social Health/ Family, friends, community	Be open and receptive, learn about others, develop a sense of family, interact more	Have close intimate relationships (bonding) Civic involvement	Focus on ecological interests Value-based relationships (team building, leadership)	Teach children family heritage Network Share relationships

			Puzzles, language skills, music—use your brain in different ways Left brain/ right brain Inductive and deductive reasoning	
Intellectual Health/ Education, lifelong learning, personality, special talents	Seek more education, experience life	Develop frames of reference for emotional control, self-expression, and logic		Share your wisdom, memories, positive attitude,self -expression

These are examples of how you can develop your personal goals from this base.

Now it is your turn. Using Table 2 as a model, reach deep inside yourself and grab hold of your passion's interests. (You may want to refer back to your notes from the chapter, "Moving Forward.") Identify the assets that are most meaningful to you. Strategically use this table to summarize and position the values that stir the passions that move your soul. Think about which stage fits each of your answers and how you would now gather, grow, conserve, or transfer them to their next level. Use this information to tailor make your own Value/Assets Matrix in Exercise 6. Think of it as the closest you can get to painting a portrait of your soul! (Naturally, there is no need for you to fill in all the blanks—only use the strategic values categories that make sense to you. You can add the others when they become more germane to your needs.) Summarize your personal values, passions, and assets in each of the five Whole Person Concept categories. What financial, physical, spiritual, social, and intellectual assets are most important to you? Write them down in the first (Value/Asset) column of this table. Then identify how you can gather, grow, conserve, or transfer your assets. Circle the one that best represents your current position. Notice how these different value/asset classes fit together for you.

Exercise 6: Painting A Portrait Of Your Soul...Build Your Own Value/Assets Matrix

	Strategic Value Position			
Value/Asset	Gather	Grow	Conserve	Transfer
Financial Health/				
Physical Health/				
Spiritual Health/				
Social Health/				
Intellectual Health/				

You will be referring back to your answers to this exercise when you get to Chapter 7, so please take the time to complete it while it is still fresh in your mind. In the beginning, you might find it difficult summarizing your own assets—the tangible ones are easy enough, but intangible personal assets are sometimes difficult to acknowledge. Gradually, your perception of your assets will clarify over time and begin to represent each of the five areas of the Whole Person Concept. This will help you move towards your goals with greater speed and clarity than ever before.

Values, Goals, Assets, Resources

For our purposes here, we are interested only in the assets and resources that grab your attention the most. These are the ones that you have defined above, the ones that you will use to create your best future. Throughout life, you set goals and implement processes to acquire specific items that you choose either to keep or discard. In turn, the items you keep hold either subjective value (such as a ring that belonged to your favorite aunt) or objective value (such as the dollar value an appraiser might place on that ring). Based on your focus and your attitude, the old adage "one man's trash is another's treasure" applies. Assets can be hard, cold, and impersonal—like cash—or soft, warm, and cherished—like a treasured photo album. When you examine your current thoughts about an asset, be open-minded. Explore your entire perception of your "whole person." Focus only on your best answers. You are establishing your strategic position for setting your grandest life goals. You are creating the bases for achieving the future that you once only dreamt about!

Chapter 7
The Tactical Process
To Achieve Your Goals

So far you have focused on understanding the *strategic* importance of the "life values side" of your Whole Person Concept. The Goals Incubator helped you to understand how your values and your assets interact and work together. Once this strategic level is established, you have a starting point, and a strong desire, to take action to achieve your goals.

We mentioned earlier that the Goals Incubator represented the strategic side of the coin. Now it is time to flip the coin over and look at the Tactical Goal Achievement Process. To put your goal plans into action, you need a *tactical* understanding of the tools available and what is required to optimize them to achieve your goals.

Now you will be focusing on the goal implementation side of your Whole Person Concept. Your tactical process focuses each value's meaning and each asset's purpose. This is where you put all the pieces in place, so that there is no excuse for delay or failure in achieving your goal.

Depending on your goal, some tools will be more appropriate for getting results than others. Each goal will require a customized approach, but this does not mean that you must "reinvent the wheel" every time you choose a new goal to work on. You can learn from your experience. When you do this, your early attempts at goal achievement take on new meaning. As Thomas Edison said when asked about his many failures in inventing the light bulb and replied, "I have not failed. I've just found 10,000 ways that won't work."

Like Edison, we should all learn from our failures. I prefer to use a consistent process that helps you to repeat your successes and identify the causes of your failures. This is the Six-Step Tactical Goal Achievement Process I recommend:

Six-Step Tactical Goal Achievement Process

Step 1: Define/Set the Goal: This initiates the process and establishes what you want to do. The type of assets related to one set of goals will be different from those related to another; for example, a physical health goal, such as weight loss, will require different assets and resources from those required for a spiritual goal such as charitable giving.

Step 2: Collect Data: Take inventory of your assets and resources relative to your goal. This defines what resources you have available to help you to achieve the goal you are establishing.

Step 3: Assess/Evaluate Data: When you know what you have got and you know what you want, you can determine what is missing and what you need to do to get from "A" to "B." *Assess/Evaluate* refers to making critical judgments. Is your goal attainable based on your available assets and resources? As you work towards your goal, what other tools do you need to acquire? How will you acquire them?

Step 4: Plan/Recommend: Write Your Action Plan: Determine what you need to do, identify alternative courses of action and their probable outcomes, and then ultimately decide upon and document the best course of action to achieve your goal, along with your timetable and progress measurements.

Step 5: Implement Your Plan: This is where you truly establish your commitment to the goal by taking the steps necessary to put your preferred course of action into effect.

Step 6: Review Data Periodically: Here you re-confirm your goal, re-collect your data, and re-evaluate your progress. Your up-to-date information helps to measure and evaluate the success of the previously implemented program. Step 6 leads back to Steps 1 and 2—the reassessment of the goal and its achievement to date (i.e., whether it has been accomplished, next steps to take, different resources, assets or approaches to consider). Then the cycle is repeated. Through the Goal Achievement Process you determine your tactical approach regarding how you will achieve your goals. (I recommend you do this every 90 days—Chapter 12 expands upon this.)

This six-step process can be applied to every goal. It provides a consistent structure for all of your goal achievement activities. It focuses your efforts on the specific tactics and tasks required to achieve each goal. In the Goal Achievement Process, you identify available tools and techniques to help achieve your goals and enhance your values.

Let's tie all this together. We have the strategic side (Goals Incubator) and the tactical side (Goal Achievement Process). Previously, in Exercise 6, you created your Value/Asset Matrix; now we move to the next step. To recap, the Value/Asset Matrix identifies specific assets that you want to focus on and apply to gather, grow, conserve, or transfer. The actions needing to be taken become the building blocks of your Whole Person Concept. Depending on your strategic perception within the Goals Incubator, you will choose tools specific to your goal. Just as a carpenter knows when to use a hammer rather than a screwdriver, you will choose the appropriate tools, too. Of course, if you try hard enough, you can use a screwdriver to remove a nail and you can use a hammer to drive in a screw. But if you use the appropriate tools for their intended purpose, you will get the job done with less effort and better results.

Here, you can begin to think about your values and your assets differently. You can identify which stage you are at for each one. Before you had this understanding, if someone asked you about "your assets," you might have limited your response to your most liquid financial assets, such as investments, retirement funds, and short-term savings. Less liquid assets might follow, including your home, car, artwork, jewelry, furs, collections, and life insurance policies. In an emergency, you might tap into their value by either selling or placing them as collateral for a loan.

Now thinking from the perspective of the Whole Person Concept, you would no longer stop here. You know that you have other valuable assets that make you unique—your physical, social, spiritual, and intellectual states of health are all priceless assets.

Ask yourself this question: "If I could only have four of my five Whole Person Concept asset categories, which one would I be willing to give up?"

★ Financial assets?

★ Physical health?

★ Spiritual peace of mind?

★ Intellectual well-being?

★ Relationships with family and friends?

Typically, when faced with this type of a decision, you would never consider sacrificing your physical and mental health, your important personal relationships, or your sense of spiritual well-being just to be rich. The most frequent choice for expendability is financial assets. Your inner assets are irreplaceable. Your financial resources are there to add value. They are usually seen as the easiest to replace. Yet, financial assets are also the ones you think of first, place most of your effort in achieving, and use to evaluate the worth of other items. This does not mean that your financial assets are any less important, rather, and most significantly, *it is through how you use your financial assets that you enhance the value of all your other, more important, assets.*

Financial assets have a special value in that they enhance all the other assets. You use your financial assets to maintain and improve your physical health, to expand your mental capabilities, to enhance your key personal relationships, or to support your favorite charities. Nonetheless, most people are more often willing to forego their financial assets to keep any and all of the others.

At this point, we need to pull together our strategic and tactical views of the five asset categories and begin to identify what goals we want to set. Physical health, spirituality, intellect, and loving relationships are impossible to replace. So let's focus first on those irreplaceable assets.

Physical Health

Physical Health is one of the key dimensions that makes you unique and different from each of the other 7 billion human beings on the planet. Physical Health is about more than just muscle and a sense of wellness. It includes the efficiency of your five senses and the ability of your various physical organ systems (respiratory, circulatory, lymphatic, digestive, reproductive, and so on) to perform effectively. Your Physical Health reflects how your body functions—with and without your conscious effort.

You can proactively change your Physical Health. How? You can enhance your health and delay the aging process through diet and exercise. However, you will age and as you grow older, your perception of acceptable Physical Health changes. As you go from building health, to maintaining your strength, to losing muscle tone, your ideal definition of healthy well-being may not change—*but your expectations of how you experience health will.* The temporary aches and pains of a child hold much different significance than the chronic conditions of the elderly.

The strategic goals for Physical Health, which you set through your Goals Incubator, affect you at every age. To optimize your health, your assets include developing good habits, such regular exercise and a healthy diet, and eliminating bad ones, such as smoking and excessive drinking or recreational drug use. The diet you choose affects how your body processes food and stores energy. Unhealthy food can leave residue in your body, which accumulates and creates side effects—like cancer and heart attacks—later in life. While you gather, grow, and conserve your Physical Health, you can also transfer your healthy habits to your children and others or transfer (eliminate) part of your weight and toxins through exercise.

In their recent books, *Younger Next Year*[3] and *Younger Next Year for Women*,[4] Chris Crowley and Dr. Harry Lodge offer a strategy for a lifestyle that offsets the effects of aging and adds vitality to your life. Their 10-step process includes aerobic and anaerobic exercise, adequate rest, sleep, diet, and passionate interests in your life.

Your Physical Health Goal Achievement Process includes diet, strength, leisure activities, and endurance. Physical Health includes not only keeping your body at a level of optimum health, but also being able to maximize your ability to experience with your senses. Leisure is important to your Physical Health. Leisure helps you to recharge your batteries and take more opportunities to find enjoyment in life.

Tactically, Physical Health goals can be divided into two activity levels:

1. **Basic Activities:** Eat a balanced diet, get adequate rest, exercise to build muscle and stamina, and practice proper hygiene to minimize infection and disease.

2. **Advanced Activities:** Develop habits that encourage structural flexibility, eliminate toxins, and balance your metabolism. Set a good example in your health habits to transfer your values to the next generation.

---

[3] Chris Crowley and Harry S. Lodge, *Younger Next Year: A Guide to Living Like 50 Until You're 80 and Beyond.* New York: Workman Publishing, 2004.
[4] Chris Crowley and Harry S. Lodge, *Younger Next Year: For Women.* New York: Workman Publishing, 2005.

Enhance these fundamental levels and you will also enhance many of the automatic functions of your body, too.

Table 3: Physical Health

Strategic Value	Description/ Value	Detail/Asset	Strategic Goal	Tactical Goal
Gather	Develop good health habits	Diet, rest, weight control	Build strong, healthy body	Balanced diet Sleep/ Re-energize
Grow	Build strength	Hygiene, exercise	Build stamina	Hygiene Anaerobic/ aerobic exercise
Conserve	Maintain health	Flexibility, detoxifica-tion	Eliminate disease	Lifestyle habits i.e. eliminating toxicities and system cloggers, improving flexibility and balance
Transfer	Teach good health habits to others	Role model for good habits	Share wisdom	Metabolic balance Role modeling

Physical Health goals will take on different meanings at various life stages. Given your current age and physical condition, what do you see as positive steps you can take now to create a brighter, more satisfying sense of physical well-being? To help set your perspective on your Physical Health, answer the Mind-Stretcher Question in Exercise 7.

Exercise 7: Physical Health Mind-Stretcher Answers

If your success were guaranteed, what Physical Health goals would you strive to achieve over the next three years?

1._____

2._____

3._____

Now, please mark the order of importance of these three goals to you.

Spiritual Health (Well-Being)

For many people, Spiritual Health equates to religious belief. To others, it refers to the inner grounding by which they live their lives. Because our focus is on your goal setting and goal achieving in this book, we define Spiritual Health as referring to how you perceive yourself and your role in relation to creation—to what has come before and what will come after you. This is not about which religious beliefs are most correct. Our focus here is on how you relate to your beliefs in order to create congruency in your life, and what goals you intend to set for yourself. Important questions fall along the following lines: What are your ethics and your sense of morality? How do you cope with the day-to-day stresses of personal interaction? Do you distinguish between morality and ethics? Is there a difference in how you treat yourself, or your immediate circle of family and friends, and how you treat others? Do you have a concept of God? Of a power greater than you? Of destiny? Of a hereafter? Of right and wrong? Your answers are your assets and the resources that you find strength in during a time of need.

Spiritual questions include more than "Who am I?" "Why am I here?" "What is expected of me?" "What legacy do I want to leave the world?" With Spiritual Health, you have an inner sense of peace that comes with faith. How do you establish and maintain that peace of mind and re-establish your grounding? Conviction in your beliefs is something you gather from your parents, teachers, peers, and your life experiences. It is through your personal experience that you grow your spiritual well-being to a higher level—so high that there is no need to conserve your Spiritual Health, because your spiritual well-being can be limitless. You strive to transfer your convictions to your children, to share your values, and preserve your traditions in the next generation.

Spiritual Health involves your senses of morality and mortality, your philosophy of life, your sense of faith, and belief in a power greater than yourself. It encompasses how you establish and maintain peace of mind through prayer, meditation, and other forms of spiritual exercise. Typical Spiritual Health goals involve enhancing your relationship with the Divine, leading a more moral life, and increasing peace of mind. Tactics might include activities like studying spiritual writings, praying, associating with like-minded people, or volunteering to help others.

Tactically, Spiritual Health goals focus on creating peace of mind, religious experience, and developing a personal philosophy. They can be divided into two levels of activities:

1. **Basic Activities:** Read inspirational and philosophical books, share ideas, pray, volunteer, and focus on ethical and moral acts. Demonstrate your conviction of what is right and wrong.

2. **Advanced Activities:** Meditate and associate with like-minded people. When you live according to your beliefs, you have faith in your life and seek the best in others. Set a good example in your spiritual health habits to transfer your values to the next generation.

No need to skimp in the Spiritual Health area. Hoarding your spirituality does not make you better; living it and sharing it does. The great thing about assets/resources such as Spiritual Health is that they are self-replenishing. The more you share them, the more you have left.

Table 4 summarizes these points regarding your Spiritual Health.

Table 4: Spiritual Health

Strategic Value	Description/ Value	Detail/Asset	Strategic Goal Area	Tactical Goal Area
Gather	Know what is right	Do what is right, read, talk, listen, pray	Do what is right	Read religious or philosophical works Attend church, listening, prayer
Grow	Live your spirituality —help others	Volunteer, act ethically and morally	Improve the world by your actions and example	Charitable work Focus on ethical, moral acts
Conserve	Spirituality has no limits	Meditate, associate with like-minded people Live your faith	Develop a sense of inner peace	Meditate Find inspiration
Transfer	Role modeling	Teach others about responsibility, right and wrong, "walk your talk" by doing good works	The "Pay it forward" idea	Observe, become role model "Random acts of kindness"

Next, from a spiritual perspective, answer the Mind-Stretcher Question in Exercise 8.

Exercise 8: Spiritual Health Mind-Stretcher Answers

If your success were guaranteed, what Spiritual Health goals would you strive to achieve over the next three years?

1._____

2._____

3._____

Now, please prioritize the order of importance of these three goals to you.

Social Health/Relationships

You are a social being. You need to interact with other people to define yourself. Yes, there is more than how you react to others' opinion of you. You can still feel good about yourself even when others might not always like you. Your high self-esteem can project leadership capabilities to others and even cause them to be attracted to you. There are steps you take to manage your relationships. There are levels of relationship and resultant responsibilities—intimate, family, social, societal. Aside from one's societal duties, responsibilities, and obligations, there are also the relationships that you want to maintain and improve upon and the ones that you are prepared to let languish.

Social interaction implies many levels and directions. There is the me-to-you (inward–outward) direction and there is the you-to-me (outward–inward) direction at the primary level. From that point, it multiplies into how I react to the way you reacted, etc. At first you may find it conceptually challenging to differentiate between the inner dimension of social interaction (the psychological and physiological dimensions of how it affects "me") and the outer dimension (the interactive, reciprocal dimensions of how "I" influence others). *Note:* Because we are looking at setting social relationship goals, our intention here is to focus primarily on the psychological dimension of "how it affects me and what I'm going to do, or how I'm going to react to it." Although this may seem contradictory, remember that we discussed earlier that you can only set a goal for yourself. Consequently, for our purposes with each of the Whole Person Concept categories, it is necessary to limit your attention to what affects you and what goals you are going to set to improve how you relate to your spouse or children or your supervisor or your customers. You cannot control or direct how others relate to you, but you *do* control how you relate to them.

Whether intentional or not, every relationship you have develops its own history, is eventually affected by this history, and comes complete with its own baggage. Every relationship has two sides, yours and the other person's. Every interest implies a sense of entitlement—that is, "What I can expect to get from you just because I'm me." Sometimes people forget about the other half: "What you can expect to get from me just because you're you." Successful relationships are built on the "you" side more than the "me" side. The point here is, what are you going to do to maintain or improve your half of the relationship—without expectation and with patience and openness? When a relationship starts to languish, the key question should be "What are you going to do about it?" If the relationship is important to you, how will you put aside your sense of entitlement to preserve it? Sometimes it can be as easy to start by saying "Thank you" or "I'm sorry" with openness, or by friendly eye contact and a smile. Other times there will be a need to clear away years of hurt to rekindle former warmth and intimacy. In short, for a relationship to be healthy, it needs to involve the best interests of the participants in recipro-cal interactions. When one person's interests dominate, the rela-tionship becomes unhealthy. Whatever the objective, it all starts with you.

Your relationships range in intimacy from close relationships with family members and friends, to the more impersonal ones with neighbors, co-workers, supervisors, suppliers, and clients. These relationships all reflect your range of influence in the world. Leadership, delegation, and leverage are dimensions of your range of influence and of your ability to build a team work-ing on your ideas.

You also have other impersonal relationships through your participation in the larger society. Among other activities, you participate in society in many ways such as obeying laws, voting, and paying taxes.

Throughout your life, you gather more social health into your sphere of influence. When the chemistry is right, you grow rela-tionships to a higher level. You conserve by nurturing key rela-tionships so that they will last. There are times when you want to see key relationships expand to include younger family members and friends as you transfer your sphere of influence to others. There are also times when you might have unintentionally let a relationship dwindle. (Please refer back to Exercise 3 in Chapter 2 about keeping the spark alive.)

You also have social responsibilities to those around you. These include your contributions to the civic, legal, and financial needs of society, ranging from voting to recycling and reducing your energy consumption.

So, many individuals set goals to improve their relationships with specific family members, friends, and co-workers. They also establish goals to give back to society for the benefit they have received.

Tactically, Social Health goals therefore focus on three levels: family, friends and acquaintances, and the society in which you live.

1. **Basic Activities:** Develop friendships and working relationships. Elevate these to closer, more intimate personal relationships, and demonstrate your level of participation in society as a whole (taxpayer, voter, volunteer, etc.).

2. **Advanced Activities:** Take an active leadership role to conserve your interests and protect the environment; act as mentor or role model. Create, develop, and hand down family, cultural, and social heritage from generation to generation. Share your history to build a path for the next generation. In some societies, family heads create an "ethical will" to transfer their values to the next generation.

Table 5 summarizes these points regarding your Social Health.

Table 5: Social Health/Relationships

Strategic Value	Description/ Value	Detail/Asset	Strategic Goal Area	Tactical Goal Area
Gather	Attract people to you	Be receptive, learn about others Sense of family	Make friends, share	Family, friends, co-workers, clients
Grow	Build alliances	Bond with others Become active member of society	Build intimate relationship Respect	Social responsibility—voting, civic duty Common ground-bonding
Conserve	Strengthen friendships and contribution, leverage	Value-based friendships Ecological considerations Leadership and team building	Stay married, preserve	Set an example of leadership, team building Ecological interests
Transfer	Influence futures	Network, share relationships, teach children	Refer your advisors, share family heritage with other family members	Mentor Pass down your family's heritage to the next generation

Based upon your understanding of your Social Health, please respond to the Mind-Stretcher Question in Exercise 9.

Exercise 9: Social Health Mind-Stretcher Answers

If your success were guaranteed, what Social Health goals would you strive to achieve over the next three years?

1._____

2._____

3._____

Remember, you can only set a goal for yourself, not for others!

Now, please mark the order of importance of these three goals to you.

Intellectual Health

Intellectual Health encompasses your intellectual capabilities and how you use them. Assets include how you think and learn and what life experience and education you have accumulated. What about your habits, memories, aspirations, and wisdom? Your imagination? How do you process information and respond to stress? How do you understand and cope with life?

Your Intellectual Health also includes what you know, how you add to that storehouse of knowledge, and how you deal with information. Intellectual Health involves your conscious and subconscious mind, your ego, and other dimensions of personality necessary for private and interpersonal interaction.

You gather experience and expertise throughout your life. You grow your intellectual resources and resourcefulness through your life experience and education. When you find yourself in a new situation, you search your psyche for signposts where you dealt with similar situations in the past, or you might role model based upon your observations of others whom you admire. You conserve your mental capacity and memories as you age, and you seek to transfer your knowledge to others who are important to you.

Preservation of your family's culture and values is in your hands. You have lived through one of the most challenging and dynamic periods in world history, and you have accomplished much in your life. You have learned lessons and developed values that you want your children, grandchildren, and theirs to know and emulate. You need to share your values, knowledge, and resourcefulness with future generations of your family.

Intellectual Health includes how you assimilate new learning and develop new knowledge, wisdom, and the vision that keeps you energized and connected to the world around you. Intellectual Health goals include developing new resources and capabilities, overcoming or developing specific habits, or responding to situations in a different way.

Tactically, Intellectual Health goals focus on lifelong learning, personality, and special talents:

1. **Basic Activities:** Seek new experiences and education, both formal and informal. Demonstrate emotional self-control and practice common sense.

2. **Advanced Activities:** Develop your brain with new challenges. If you think of the brain as a muscle, you can also perceive the need to exercise it to keep it working at peak efficiency. You shift from left-brain to right-brain activities when you learn a new language, solve puzzles, write, or take up a musical instrument. Use your logic, both inductive and deductive—even you can be Sherlock Holmes! Think positively and learn how to release your mind from negative thoughts and images.

Table 6 summarizes these points regarding your Intellectual Health.

Table 6: Intellectual Health

Strategic Value	Description/ Value	Detail/Asset	Strategic Goal Area	Tactical Goal Area
Gather	Have experiences	Be open to new experiences, learn	Develop an education	Education New experiences
Grow	Develop deductive and inductive reasoning	Generalize from experiences to control emotions and develop common sense	Make sound decisions	Emotional control Common sense
Conserve	Exercise your brain	Puzzles, language skills, music: using your brain in different ways	Preserve your ability to remember	Deductive and inductive reasoning Problem solving/language, music (left brain/right brain)
Transfer	Share values, preserve history Inheritance Communicate	Share your wisdom, memories, cultural heritage Stay positive Know your roots and anchors	Share heritage with younger family members	Receive positive messages Self-expression Share your wisdom

From an intellectual perspective, answer the Mind-Stretcher Question in Exercise 10.

Exercise 10: Intellectual Health Mind-Stretcher Answers

If your success were guaranteed, what Intellectual Health goals would you strive to achieve over the next three years?

1._____

2._____

3._____

Now, please prioritize the order of importance of these three goals to you.

Financial Health

Financial Health addresses how you exchange value (including money) with others. Your financial assets help you use and benefit from your other assets. In many instances, Financial Health is your starting point for gathering, growing, conserving, and transferring your other assets. Physical Health can be enhanced by hiring a trainer or buying better quality food. Spiritual Health might include giving to charity or paying for spiritual development seminars and retreats. Social Health involves going places and doing things with others—creating experiences and memories to share. Intellectual Health might require investing in tutoring or coaching, classes, or books.

Money is just a tool—it is neither good nor bad. Like any tool, it is how you use it that counts. Some people see money as plentiful; others consider it scarce.

You might be afraid of money and abdicate this responsibility to others. Maybe you charge major purchases—borrowing instead of waiting until you can pay cash. Maybe you hoard money or you are secretive about it. You might not be able to distinguish between investing and gambling, and risk your hard-earned retirement savings. Some even see money as a means to control people.

Or perhaps you have a handle on money and it serves you well. Maybe you seek the help of skilled professionals in tax planning, accounting, investing, and so on. Seeking professional assistance with finances is no different than getting medical, dental, or legal advice.

As your financial resources increase, you learn that you can make your financial assets work for you to grow new wealth. In time, your focus may change from creating new wealth to conserving it. Eventually you will want to share your financial wealth and transfer it to those who are important to you.

Your ability to gather, grow, and conserve financial assets affects all of these actions. Transfer of financial assets and attitudes to the next generation is also an important dimension of wealth creation.

You can also transfer your financial smarts, wealth creation habits, values, attitudes, and key advisor relationships to your successors. This aspect of transferring wealth is critical for the perpetuation of one generation's financial acuity to the next. It is equally important to create, preserve, and share lifestyle and career opportunities between generations.

Each of the five tactical areas can be seen as an end or a means to an end. Financial assets are tools to achieve other goals, not merely goals in themselves. Riches come from how you use the wealth you have rather than amassing financial wealth you will never use.

Tactically, Financial Health goal activities can be divided into two levels: basic and advanced.

1. **Basic Activities:** Budget, educate yourself about financial planning, live within your means, and control debt, to work towards your short-term goals. Long-term retirement strategies focus on the genius of compounding and the need to preserve the buying power of your money relative to inflation by investing your excess cash flow for growth.

2. **Advanced Activities:** Develop tax minimization strategies, practice estate planning and special-needs planning (to care for a dependent adult child and or fund philanthropic interests), manage risk with life, disability, and other insurance as needed.

Table 7 summarizes these points regarding your Financial Health.

Table 7: Financial Health

Strategic Value	Description/ Value	Detail/Asset	Strategic Goal Area	Tactical Goal Area
Gather	Create a financial asset reserve	Earnings exceed expenses Understand, control debt	Acquire possessions, save money	Budget Learn about finances
Grow	Compound growth preserve buying power	Invested assets grow faster than inflation, diversification	Growth wealth	Invest Protect against inflation Save for retirement Compound your savings
Conserve	Stretch value of a assets optimize savings	Minimize volatility, maximize growth, defer taxes	Makes savings last longer	Manage risk Defer taxes
Transfer	Give financial assets to children, charity, government	Joint ownership, wills, trusts, powers of attorney, insurance	Teach children how to achieve prosperity	Estate planning Insurance Special needs

Financial Health goals range from eliminating debt and controlling your finances, to building a comfortable retirement and leaving a legacy for your children rather than the taxman. Now that you have some perspective on Financial Health, take a deep breath, close your eyes, and think of what would give you a sense of improved Financial Health. Do Exercise 11 and answer the Mind-Stretcher Question for your Financial Health.

Exercise 11: Financial Health Mind-Stretcher Answers

If your success were guaranteed, what Financial Health goals would you strive to achieve over the next three years?

1._____

2._____

3._____

Now, please mark the order of importance of these three goals to you.

Summarizing Your Mind-Stretcher Goals

Now you have answered the Mind-Stretcher Question for each of the five Whole Person categories. It is time to pull your thoughts together. Please use Exercise 12 to summarize and prioritize your answers to the five Mind-Stretcher Questions in this chapter. You will be working with your answers in the chapters that follow.

Exercise 12: Prioritized Summary of Mind-Stretcher Answers

Whole Person Concept Category	First Goal	Second Goal	Third Goal
Financial Health			
Physical Health			
Spiritual Health			
Social Health			
Intellectual Health			

We will be coming back to this table again. Before going any further, please review your answers in the above table and circle the five items most important to you.

⌒

This completes Element One: Taking Stock—The Value/Asset Inventory, and Element Two: Focus—The Strategic Goal-Setting Level. In this section, you have focused on your thinking about the Whole Person Concept, the strategically oriented Goals Incubator, and the tactical Goal Achievement Process, and have begun to integrate these concepts. You have identified your major values and assets in each of the five Whole Person Concept categories. You have identified your top three priorities to achieve in each of the Whole Person Concept categories over the next three years. You have initiated the first steps towards deciding on what goals will help you to create the best future you.

In Part Three, we continue to Empowerment—The Tactical Goal Process Level, the third element of operating the Whole Person Concept. This is where you will begin to create the goals achievement processes that will include the tools fundamental to empowering you as you turn your dreams into reality. Having all the tools (assets, resources, etc.) is critical to your successful goal achievement. How many times have you started on a project only to see it get derailed by trips to the hardware store or the grocery store in quest of that one item crucial to job completion? I know that, when I look around the house, I have been challenged by jobs still on the go for just that reason! This is where we will get more systematic about our goal achievement processes. We want to ensure that we have all the tools needed to do the job so that we will optimize our time and effort and get on to the next stage of our journey.

PART THREE

Goal Setting And Goal Achieving

EMPOWER!

*Second, have the necessary means to achieve your ends:
wisdom, money, materials, and methods.*

Chapter 8
Creating Your Passion—
Aligning Your Goals With Your Values

At the start of this book, in "Moving Forward," you rediscovered your passions. In Chapter 3, you were introduced to the Whole Person Concept. In Chapter 6, you established your strategic position in the Goals Incubator for each of the five components of Whole Person Concept, and in Chapter 7, you answered the Mind-Stretcher Question establishing what outcomes need to be achieved within three years for each of your five key goal achievement processes. Now, on to the next step—connecting your Mind-Stretcher *tactical* answers with your *strategic* values and assets. Your passions, your strategic position relative to the Goals Incubator, your understanding of the Whole Person Concept, and Mind-Stretcher answers should all tie together. In this chapter, we want to make sure that they belong with each other. You could consider this as applying "quality control principles" to the data you have been accumulating. The following questions and diagram show how this will all come together.

Goals come from whatever you are most passionate about. Goal definition is a four-stage process, as illustrated in Diagram 4. You have been working through these steps as you have been progressing through the first half of this book. You have already answered questions such as "What is your passion?" and "How do you set meaningful goals aligned with your values?" Looking forward now, we are going to start moving from the theoretical level to its practical application.

Diagram 4: Goal Definition Of Four-Stage Process

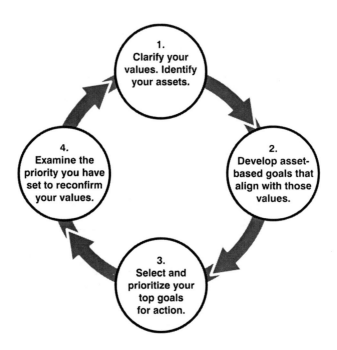

There are many great ideals that you might hold dear: freedom, loyalty, honesty, patriotism, compassion, and so on. These core values are beliefs that underlie most aspects of everyday life, yet they are larger than life. When your society's very existence is threatened, these beliefs propel you into action to serve your country and put your life at risk to protect what you hold most precious. For most, these values apply when you put your life on hold and your ideals come first. For those to whom we all owe so much, this is a daily occurrence. For the rest of us, these values may be deeper than we need to go when looking at personal goal setting. This book is more about the personal day-to-day world that you live in and that you want to create.

You need to look at the personal values that come up daily in your life "where the rubber meets the road." These values shape your goals and pave the way to the person you want to become.

For example, if you are an office worker, your continued employ-ment and career advancement might depend on certain career attributes (assets) such as efficiency, decision making, follow-up, and timeliness. At a practical level, your passion here may be connected to the benefits that job security provides for your leisure time or your personal satisfaction in the quality of the work you receive and give to others. Gathering material wealth could be defined by an immediate goal of improved punctuality so that you not only build a reputation of reliability, but also have the extra time needed to increase your work quality and accura-cy. This builds your reputation and elevates your status within your work team's environment.

Not everyone has the same values, and people often have dif-ferent reasons for holding similar values. You need to look at both aspects—what you value most *and* why.

Your values are personal anchors that you will come back to as you develop your goals. Streamlining and personalizing your values will clarify them for easier goal development and assess-ment.

A summary of these four stages follows.

Stage One: Clarify Your Values, Identify Your Assets

First, starting with what you are passionate about and what makes you feel alive, from "Moving Forward," you identified your key assets. You started with the Whole Person Concept's five basic value/asset areas (Intellectual Health, Physical Health, Spiritual Health, Social Health, and Financial Health). Exercise 6: Painting a Portrait of Your Soul...Build Your Own Value/Assets Matrix was completed in Chapter 6.

Stage Two: Aligning Goals With Values

Review your Mind-Stretcher Goals that you wrote down in Chapter 7. This was where you established what you want to accomplish over the next three years.

Stage Three: Select and Prioritize Goals That Mean The Most

Now it is time to build upon this base. Examine your responses to Chapter 7's Prioritized Summary of Mind-Stretcher Answers (Exercise 12) more closely. First, identify and focus on your overall top five goals. (Use Exercise 13 to summarize.)

Exercise 13: Top Five Items To Be Accomplished

Value/Asset Area And Mind-Stretcher Goal	What This Means To Me (My Definition)	Why It Is A Top Priority
Example for Health: Getting a good 8 hours of sleep every night	Waking up relaxed and refreshed every day	After 8 hours of sound sleep, I am more patient and attentive the next day.
A.		
B.		
C.		
D.		
E.		

At this point, you will probably have one key goal for each of the five Whole Person Concept categories. However, if you have a concentration of goals in one category, that is okay too. This might change at some point in the future. What is important now is to become sensitized to what is on the top of your mind. Use Exercise 13 to expand on each of these five future goals. What do they mean to you? Why you have given them high priority?

Go deeper into your reasoning. Ask yourself why each goal is important to you. Using the example of a good night's sleep in Exercise 13, the reason for its importance—patience and attentiveness—could lead to unexpected results such as "When I am patient and attentive, I can create warmer relationships with my spouse, family, and co-workers. This is important to me because I want others to like me. When others like me, I feel warm and appreciated." In this instance, the health goal of getting a good night's sleep is actually a social relationship goal. That might change your thinking about it and help you see how this goal is supportive of other areas in your life.

Getting a good night's sleep could also lead to the rationale of waking up alert and rested, without aches and pains. The deeper meaning here might be "When I wake up alert and rested, I have more energy and my senses are heightened. I am better able to appreciate the splendor of the world around me and to give praise to God for even the littlest things in my life." Here, your health goal is spiritual as well. The clearer you can get about your deepest motivation for these top five goals, the stronger your confidence and commitment to them. With this new understanding of your top five answers, move the answers into Exercise 14. Examine them from an operational point of view. Identify the assets and resources required to achieve your three-year Mind-Stretcher Goals. You will probably need to acquire additional assets or resources. Use Exercise 14 to make a note about that in the last column so you know what you need to do. Having all the assets, resources, tools, etc., that you can identify as being necessary to achieve your goal is basic to your sense of empowerment. The summary of missing assets/resources becomes your shopping list. You need these to properly empower your Goal Achievement Process.

Exercise 14: Integrating Goals And Assets

Whole Person Category	Answers To The Mind-Stretcher Question	Assets Required	Assets Required	Shortfall In Assets
Example: Physical Health	I want to tighten up my stomach muscles	Time Discipline Exercise routine Tracking system Trainer	Time Discipline	Exercise routine Tracking system Trainer
A.				
B.				
C.				
D.				
E.				

Stage Four: Re-Examine Priorities And Reconfirm Values

You are making great progress! You are gaining a deeper understanding of your goals than most people ever achieve! You are becoming an elite goal setter. You are linking your values, assets, and goals. Goals tend to fall into two general categories: (a) enhancing something you already have (pleasure) or (b) preventing something you want to avoid (pain). If you think about this visually, it is a lot like an old-fashioned scale with a tipping point—the point where things change: add extra weight on one side and the scale drops in that direction. The balance point represents the equilibrium where you need neither to enhance (add) nor eliminate (subtract).

Just about everything has a tipping point where it balances between one status and another. If you think about the temperature of a room, there is a balance point where you are just comfortable—neither hot nor cold. When the temperature moves outside your comfort zone, you become more motivated to take action to re-establish your comfort zone. Depending on the circumstance, you want to turn the temperature either up or down. There is a basic four-step sequence that you go though in this type of situation. Table 8 summarizes these four steps and compares them to the four elements identified at the end of Chapter 4.

Table 8: Tipping Point Sequence

Tipping Point Model	Our Four-Element Model
1. Although formerly you were content within your comfort zone, now you realize that something has changed	**Element One:** *Taking Stock*—**The Value/Asset Inventory.** This establishes your current status (what you already have-your assets and resources).
2. You are outside of your comfort zone and concentrating on what action to take	**Element Two:** *Focus*—**The Strategic Goal-Setting Level.** Based on your awareness of your resources and your preconceived values, you decide what you want to do. (your goal).
3. After assessing your situation and resources, you decide on the correct action to take to get back into your comfort zone	**Element Three:** *Empowerment*—**The Tactical Goal Process Level.** Based on the tools at hand, a goal achievement program is developed and you implement the specific tactical process required to achieve your goals
4. You take positive action and continue to take action until you are comfortable again.	**Element Four:** *Persistence*—**Keep the Goal Foremost in Mind.** You keep working at your priority until you are comfortable again (achieve your goal)

After you become aware of the need for change, the function of controlling your tipping point employs three principles that might surprise you:

1. **Focus** is the first principle. When you focus on the desired change that is required to eliminate or create the difference between one state and another, you are aware of the need for change. The first principle, then, is *"focus."* When you define your goals and focus energy and enthusiasm on them, they catch fire and become realizable.

2. **Empowerment** is the second principle. Many goals seem overwhelming because of the magnitude of change and not knowing the steps to reach them. When you take ownership and activate your Goal Achievement Process, you gain a feeling of *"empowerment."* Empowerment means "getting it right"—right in every sense—the right time frame, the right environment, the right attitude, the right understanding of the next steps, the right tools. Empowerment is the result of eliminating all the myriad little elements that stand between you and your successful accomplishment of your goal. Either you are empowered or you are not. There is really no middle ground.

3. Persistence is the third principle. If you keep coming back and working towards your objective, the result will be different than if you flit from task to task without ever finishing things. *"Persistence"* is the feature that pulls you back to the goal over and over and over. Persistent activity on the same goal is much more effective than scattering your attention among many different points. You might think of each return to your priority as reminding yourself what needs to be done. The more you keep coming back to this same goal, the more likely you are to achieve it.

Think of your goal as balancing on that old-fashioned scale (Diagram 5) where one side equals the other. The balance point refers to where you think you are now, rather than where you want to come to be. This is your status quo in goal setting. Your objective is to create a new tipping point consistent with your new goal—to upset your old status quo so that you will take action towards your goal and never look back and return to your former "you." Every time you return to your former status quo is a step back towards the comfortable old "you" that you are familiar with and that you seek to change. Adding more weight on one side throws off the balance: the tipping point factor. For your goals, the positive "extra weight" that tips the balance is made up of the answers to your Wake-Up Call's "What the heck!?!" questions from Exercise 5.

Diagram 5: The "Wake-up Call" Balance Scales

Most people, having an inbred sense of symmetry, feel a compulsion to bring the tipping point balance back "into balance," that is, to take action to bring it back to its vertical position. But is that in your best interest? If you want to create a new standard with a different future tipping point, you need to upset the scale and even tilt the table in your favor!

Consider the many television testimonials about weight loss systems where someone has lost 50 pounds or more. Have you ever wondered about their success in keeping those 50 pounds off? If you have lost 50 pounds and want to keep it off, you need a new tipping point with a 50-pound lighter standard. Without a new standard, your old tipping point will still be there—50 pounds heavier—and, just as the scale will correct back to its balance point, so will you gradually move back to the person you were formerly.

But what if the old balance is no longer adequate and you wish to establish a new equilibrium? This is where your passion must come in. You need to visualize the scale as being on a table, where you are free to tilt the table in your favor to bring the scale in line with you new goal's expectations—regardless of what they are—and keep it there. You are free to decide where you want the tipping point to be in the future and to take steps to use that new setting as *your* standard for future assessment. This becomes your new ideal status quo.

Now, take your top five goals and look for each goal's tipping point. As you consider each goal, ask yourself the following three questions to establish your focus, create empowerment, and develop persistent follow through in regard to each goal:

1. Focus: What will I lose if I do not achieve this goal? What do I gain by successful achievement of this goal? (Pleasure or pain?)

2. Empowerment: What assets do I need? What is my plan?

3. Persistence: What steps can I take towards achieving the next stage of this goal now?

In the first column of Exercise 15, write down your goal. In the second, list the top three obstacles you will face if you do not stay **focused** on each of those priorities. These answers indicate what would not be gained, or what would be lost, if the goal were not achieved. They are also potential sources of motivation. Next, identify your top three assets, resources, or activities that will **empower** you to stay on track.

Finally, think of the memorable criteria that you can use to persistently draw yourself back to the goal that you wish to achieve. These are what make achievement of the goal meaningful and are key to your future happiness.

Exercise 15: Tipping The Balance In Your Favor

Mind-Stretcher Answers	Obstacles to Overcome/ Focus On	Day-by-Day Empowerment	Memorable Persistence
Example: Develop six-pack abdomen	1. Excess weight (can't see toes) 2. Heart attack 3. Weak joints	Desire/environment Benchmark/ monitor your daily exercise routine Create success streak Daily meal plan	Ideal weight target Visualize ideal (photos) Accountable to coach Schedule time
A.	1. 2. 3.		
B.	1. 2. 3.		
C.	1. 2. 3.		
D.	1. 2. 3.		
E.	1. 2. 3.		

Next, you need to re-level the table. Shift your tipping point to make your goals even more powerful. Create a new standard, consistent with your goal, of what will be the new tipping point—the new minimum level of acceptable result. Sharpen your focus—your resolve—by considering how important the goal is to you.

Use Exercise 16 to examine how your awareness of the tools needed and of your daily progress in baby steps will create the progressively "better you" (empowerment) that you seek. Look at what will happen immediately after you achieve your goal (pay-off for your persistence). You might describe this as simply the satisfaction of being able to stand up straight and see your toes when you look down (without leaning forward)!

Transfer your five top goals to the chart in Exercise 16. Elaborate on their importance to you, the underlying implications, and the payoff you will achieve by completing each goal. You are creating your own personal "tipping points," which will carry you from repeated failure to focus, to being empowered, and to persistently develop success habits that carry you towards your goal achievement.

You might not see your true payoff the first time you work with this chart. It is easy to get stuck in daily living and lose sight of the compelling reasons for your bigger goals. That is okay. It might take some hard work digging through your implications to find your true payoff.

Keep working on this until you are happy with your values and goal statements. Look more closely at your big payoffs. Do you find a common theme running through them? This is no accident. This theme is your passion, your dominant motivation—the principle standing behind each value that keeps you moving forward. Your dominant motivation might surprise you at first, but as you think about it, you will understand why it drives you. Discovering your dominant motivation is a major step forward!

Exercise 16: My Top Five Goals And Their Rationale

Goal	Importance To Me (Focus)	Implication (Empowerment)	Payoff (Persistency)
Example: Get 8 hours of sound sleep every night.	With a good night's sleep, I'm more patient and attentive the next day.	When I'm patient and attentive, I can create closer relationships with my spouse, family and co-workers.	Important because I want others to like me. When others like me, I feel warm and appreciated (secure).
A.			
B.			
C.			
D.			
E.			

FINALLY—Where It All Starts: Setting A Goal

Okay, now you are thinking: "Hey, I've been at this for dozens of pages. I've spent a lot of my time doing the exercises and now I'm getting pumped. I've identified my passions! I know what my goals are. I'm ready to go! Why wait to talk about setting goals until now?"

This is a great question and it deserves an equally great answer. There is a method to my madness. Go back to the idea of the "tipping point" for a moment. People fail at goal achievement for several reasons, but the biggest include the following: Poor Strategy and Poor Tactics.

A. Poor Strategy:

★ Poorly stated goals that lack focus. (See S.M.A.R.T. goals definition below under "Poor Tactics.")

★ Lack of empowerment. Why write a terrific goal statement that is technically perfect and then decide that it is not the right goal? I want you to get the goal topic down first so that your goal statement is bulletproof and you are committed to it. Your goal statement must be "actionable." Part of empowerment is making sure that you have the resources and capability to make it happen.

★ Lack of persistent follow-up. This is critical area that we will address soon. Either you are working on your goal or on something that really isn't your goal. You need to know the difference!

You have been focusing your efforts thus far on addressing these "big three" strategic reasons for failure at goal achievement. Goal setting boils down to the same basic points.

B. Poor Tactics:

Every goal must have an operable ("the what you do") level. A goal is best understood and achievable when it is clearly and positively stated in writing, important to you, and S.M.A.R.T:

★ Specific
★ Measurable
★ Achievable
★ Realistic
★ Timely

Try this to get a feel for it. Simply write down one of your goals such as "I want to get in shape." Then write it down again, but this time try to be more specific. Keep writing it down until it makes sense to you. Now, this is not like having to write back in third grade, "I will not pull Betty's hair" 25 times. (Well, maybe you did not have to do this in third grade, but I got really good at it!) Writing down your goals takes conscious effort. You need to work and rework through your thoughts to clarify exactly what you mean so that you can actually implement your Goal Achievement Process.

For example, "I want to get in shape" can evolve this way:

★ I want to lose 25 pounds before Thanksgiving.

★ I want to reduce my weight from 175 to 150 pounds between June 1st and November 1st.

★ I want to reduce my weight by five pounds each month for the next five months.

★ Through regular, daily exercise of briskly walking for 30 minutes every morning before breakfast and a balanced diet of not more than 1800 calories a day, I HAVE reduced my weight by five pounds a month for each of the PAST five months. I AM IN THE HABIT OF monitoring and recording my progress and results every day. I FEEL GREAT!

As you restate your goal and flex your goal-setting muscles, your goal gets more specific. You get clearer on the steps you need to take. You visualize your success and you commit yourself to the effort. You take ownership of achieving your goal.

You must be able to picture the outcome, whether it is a "six-pack" abdomen like you see in TV infomercials or a photo of you surrounded by the smiling faces of your family. The more vivid and memorable the picture, the easier it is to stay on course.

Set Empowering Benchmarks

Can your goal be broken down into stages? Progressive bench-marks tied to specific dates empower you to achieve the next stage in your big goal.

Can your progress be quantified, measured, and monitored?

How do you set benchmarks? Let's go back to the "six-pack abs" example. Assume you want to start by doing sit-ups. How many can you do now? That is your starting point. If you are at 20 sit-ups and your goal is to do 46 sit-ups, estimate how long you think it will take. If you add one more sit-up to your daily regi-men every week, you would need 26 weeks to get to your 46 sit-ups goal. Set a benchmark at 33 sit-ups, and a progress review date of 13 weeks from now.

Do a reality check. Is this goal important to you? Do you think it will move you towards your desired outcome? Is your course of action likely to lead you to your objective? Can you do it? Are you *willing* to do it? Do you have a tracking method? Does it fit into your daily schedule? Will you monitor your progress? If the answer is "yes" to all, then you are ready to go for it! If there is a "no" in any of your answers, then rethink (*re*-focus), recon-sider (*re*-empower), and rework (*re*-persist) your commitment to your new goal. It might be someone else's goal for you, not your own. When you take ownership of your goal, you will truly enjoy achieving it. Your consistent process will become your persistent habit. Your habit is what you do to achieve your goal. Your goal is the result of the habit, not the habit.

Falling Off The Wagon

Will you "fall off the wagon and miss a day?" Probably. Is this the end of the world? Not necessarily. When a child is building a block tower and another child comes along and knocks the tower over, it is not the end of the world. What do you say? "That's okay! Build another one! Build a better one!" Give yourself the same advice and encouragement. When you miss a day, it all depends on what you do next. Do you simply accept the break in your routine as a "break" and start over, or do you beat yourself up because you failed to live up to your expectations? Do yourself a big favor—do not beat yourself up. You are worth more. You can do it. Your goal is worthwhile. When you take a break from your goal, just reassess, regroup, and start over. Learn from your actions and your attitude. Discover the reason why you took the break. Was it a day or two? A week? Longer? Did you miss your goal activity? Were you aware that you were not doing your goal activity? Were you making excuses to yourself for not doing it? ("I'm too busy. I need today off. I'll get back at it tomorrow.") When you started again, did you have a comfortable feeling like a visit with an old friend or a familiar song from your younger days?

Psychologists say it takes 21 consecutive days of consistent performance to create a habit. It also takes 21 days to change a habit. So, for daily sit-ups to become a habit, you know what you have to do. What happens on Day 22? Just congratulate yourself, measure your progress, and keep going—not letting yourself return to the old habit of doing no sit-ups. Instead, reconfirm your commitment to your new self—and raise the bar. Consider your 21-day effort to be a "winning streak" of unbroken accomplishment. Test yourself! How long a streak can you maintain? Once you break it, can you start a longer one?

Use the secret of "the game within the game" to push your success forward. Hockey legend Gordie Howe created his own "game within the game" to make practices more tolerable. Never a big fan of repetitive drills, it's said that Howe set his own target to improve his skills in ways important to him (like taking every shot to the top left corner for this practice and top right for the next one) and incorporated this into the team drills. In this way, he could hone his skills while still participating as a team player. Use the "Game Within the Game" as your motivator.

Remember, there is a difference between setting a goal and achieving it. Setting the goal is "the start" (your focus). The method you use to achieve the goal (your empowerment) that leads to creating and monitoring the goal-achieving habit is "the process" (your persistency). When the process breaks down, it does not mean the goal is unachievable. It simply means the process or the method needs work. To truly empower your goal, you might need to fine-tune your activities, or update your commitment to the goal, or measure and monitor your process activities on a daily basis, or allow time to establish a lifestyle change, or acknowledge that plateaus in your performance will happen.

There is an old adage that "if you keep doing things the same way, you'll keep getting the same results." Are you willing to get off the plateau and move up to your next level? Go back to the basic points of goal setting and start again!

How else can you ensure your success? What is your weak point regarding a specific goal? Who knows you better than you do? Then who knows the best excuses you can come up with to scuttle your goal achievement ship? When you identify your best excuses in advance, you will be better ready to win the fight between your good intentions and your not-so-good excuses—your demotivators. When you are equipped with an inside track on your best motivators and your top demotivators, you are better prepared to keep the vision of your goal "new" and alive. Use Exercise 17 to summarize the things most likely to derail your best efforts and how you will get going again.

Exercise 17: Your Goal Motivators and Demotivatorse

Tactical Goal	Your Best Excuse For Scuttling Your Own Ship (Demotivator)	Your Game Within The Game (Motivator)
1.		
2.		
3.		
4.		
5.		

Armed with this insight, you are better prepared than you have ever been to make sure you stay motivated and stick with your resolve to achieve the goals that you have set for yourself. You have even identified your most likely reasons for failure and the steps that you can take to overcome them.

Can You Create A Habit For Someone Else?

If a habit is the process you use to achieve a goal, then it should be obvious you can only create a goal process for yourself. You can create a favorable environment for goal achievement to help someone else change, but you can only establish habits for yourself. As they say, you can lead a horse to water but you can't make him drink. You can only create the opportunity!

Here's an example. If you do the family grocery shopping and you want to change your family's eating habits, you stop buying sweets and purchase fruit and veggies instead. Will this keep your kids from eating cookies? No, but they'll need to get proactive about their cookie addiction! And if they try the fruit at hand, they might just like it. A new habit could be formed! Do you see that your role is creating an environment (i.e., empowerment) that favors your desired result?

Remember disempowerment, the opposite of empowerment, is really self-sabotage. As I said earlier, empowerment is establishing and completing all the little things necessary to keep you accomplishing the baby steps towards your goals.

Is Your Vision Big Enough?

As noted earlier, creating a new habit takes 21 days of consistent performance. Consider each 21-day period as an opportunity to move progressively towards a greater goal. Your goals will be much bigger than 21 days' effort, but how big should they be?

Make them BIG! ◆

How big? As big as your whole life. When your goals combine with your ideals, you can create an unbelievable future for yourself. You create a life congruent with your values and a lifestyle that allows you to create your best future for your best self.

Typically, people are more comfortable with setting a three-month, six-month, or twelve-month goal—the equivalent of one seasonal or annual cycle. You are probably comfortable in thinking that far ahead. You can "see" three to twelve months as a time period that is realistic and achievable. Setting three-year, five-year, or ten-year goals is a bigger stretch and could tax your comfort and credulity. It takes effort to set goals over a longer time period with conviction; however, with practice, you can do it.

Stretch your imagination! Start with your one-year goal. What if you stretch your comfort level and go a step further? Can you take your one-year goal and extend it to create a three-year goal? (Remember the Mind-Stretcher Questions you answered earlier?) How about a five-year goal? If you persistently worked on the same goal for five years, imagine the progress you would achieve! Would your progress be linear? Possibly. Would you exceed your expectations by achieving your target values sooner? Probably. Should you revisit your goal and "raise the bar?" Absolutely! Mastery waits for you when you apply focused effort and movement towards your big, "reach for the stars" goals. It can take the creation of a lot of new habits to achieve a five-year goal!

But what if you miss? What if you do not achieve your five-year goal? Will you be better off than if you had never started? Most likely! The goal (focus) was not wrong; it was the level of commitment, or the timetable (empowerment), or perhaps the tracking measurement (persistence). This is why it is important to break down your goal into small, measurable, manageable mini-goal stages. As you complete each stage, you are moving forward towards the greater goal. You can also review, reassess, and revise the next stage if you need to. When revising your goal process, you reaffirm your original target and the reason you wanted to achieve it more than anything else.

If you can set and achieve a five-year goal, what is stopping you from tackling a longer time period? One of the biggest obstacles can be establishing the vision—the ability to comprehend "time." Most parents are comfortable with the idea that a newborn baby will mature into an adult and become fully independent in about 20 to 25 years. You know this will happen; you see it around you all the time. Great-grandparents have seen the cycle many times. But you do not need to be a great-grandparent to perceive and understand this cycle of maturation as it applies to your goals. You see it every day just by observing other people. So take advantage of this new insight and apply it to setting and defining your own goals. (If you love music, how old will you be in five years if you take piano lessons...?)

In the example of striving to have six-pack abs, say you began at 20 sit-ups with a goal of achieving 46 sit-ups a day in another 26 weeks. Even by missing a few days, most people will achieve the target of 46 sit-ups within half a year if they keep at it. In five years, just one extra sit-up a week (52 per year) adds up to 260 sit-ups a day. Is this an unrealistic target after five years? Are you five years away from those "six-pack" abs? Realistic? Achievable? Desirable? Someplace along the line you might say, "Yea, that's all fine, but 260 sit-ups a day! Give me a break!" Recall that when you are projecting forward like this, the process is not linear. You are free to modify your process and your goal. You are free to say, "That's enough" and to plateau. You are free to separate and redefine your Physical Health goal. It is your new habit. Make it a good one!

Remember, you are free to create the new future that you want. It is up to you to do it.

Act With Congruency

What does *congruency* mean and what does it have to do with goal setting? Here, we are using *congruency* to mean "all going in the same direction." If all your activities are leading towards the same end, then they are congruent. They are in harmony. There is a uniformity in what you are doing that works to support itself. Congruency adds strength to your goal activities and hastens your movement towards establishing your processes, achieving your goals, enhancing your assets, and perfecting your values. The healthy living we used earlier is an easy example to illustrate, so we will stay with that. If you are working towards your sit-ups goal, but drinking a six-pack a day, eating a diet high in fats and carbohydrates, and otherwise leading a couch potato lifestyle, what impact do you think this will have on achieving your 46 sit-up target? Will you still achieve your target? Possibly. Will you miss your key dates? Probably. Will you constantly struggle with your motivation? Most likely. Why? Because you are sabotaging your best intentions. You need to reaffirm and demonstrate your commitment to your goal in your daily life. So whose value is it? Whose goal are you working towards? Whose lifestyle process are you living? Is it your goal or is it someone else's? Tough question. Tougher decision. Take action! It is all about your empowerment!

This is where congruency comes in. The more you act in a consistent and congruent manner, the easier it will be to adopt lifestyle habits that support your goals and values. So, *keep your goal front and center in your mind.* Know what you need to do today to stay consistent with your desire and work towards that outcome.

Focus!

Empower!

Persist!

Monitor Your Self-Talk

Can you be outwardly congruent but inwardly not? Yes, but this leads to stress as your self-esteem falls victim to your conscience. As Pinocchio's buddy, Jiminy Cricket, said, "Let your conscience be your guide."

If you are like most people, you engage in mental self-talk—the little voice that keeps you company when you are not otherwise involved. This voice tells you many things, including whether your actions are congruent with your values. *Monitor your self-talk.* Make sure it is consistent with what you want to hear. Your subconscious is listening too, and it cannot tell the difference between fact and fiction. So your self-talk is critical to keeping you on target.

Self-talk is a lot like a spell-check program on your computer—it sits in the background waiting for you to type something that it does not agree with. Programmable in several languages, you can set your spell-checker to accept incorrectly spelled words and foreign words. Your spell-checker only recognizes patterns; it does not make value judgments. And it does not know the difference between *right, rite, write, and Wright!*

Your self-talk works in the same way. You can program it to be positive or negative, supportive or self-destructive. It is entirely up to you to monitor and modify your self-talk to suit your needs—after all, who else can possibly do this? *Only you can hear it!*

Your morning self-talk might sound like this: "I don't want to get up. Too early. Just five minutes more. Oh, I'm stiff. Oops! Got to go to the bathroom—hurry!" During the day, it might shift to "I'm not good at math. I hate giving speeches. Bet this is a piece of that new 'low-calorie chocolate cake' so I'll eat it and do two extra sit-ups…." Sometimes, you use self-talk to set expectations, make compromises or excuses, and set limits for yourself. But it does not have to be this way. You can train your self-talk to focus on the big picture and keep your wants and actions congruent with your goals. Program your self-talk to be a good navigator. As you discover that your self-talk is leading you in a direction that is not congruent with your values and goals, redirect it where you want to go. Use a daily period of quiet time to listen to your self-talk and re-program it.

Remember, like a spell-check program, your subconscious does not distinguish between fact and fiction. Only your conscious mind can do that, but it relies on your subconscious for advice and direction regarding many things such as what to expect, how you should behave, and how you should act and react.

One good way to change, is to adopt a "no negatives" habit. Do not permit your self-talk to be negative or to put you down. When you only allow positive, constructive self-talk, you will find life more enjoyable. Progressively, your attitude will become more positive and constructive. Start by addressing the phantom "they," as in "*they* should do something about that" or "*they* all think that I am fat." There are no "other people" in your subconscious—just you. It is your sanctuary—a refuge for you now and for the future you, too. Fill your self-talk with constructive, positive, empowering, future-focused words, the pronouns *I and me*, and the adjective *my*. Leave *they, them, someone,* and *somebody* to the excuse makers who are unwilling to accept responsibility for their own future. You can rise above that!

One extreme but effective method you can use to establish the "no negatives" habit is a minor form of "shock" therapy. Place an elastic band comfortably around your wrist. Every time you find a negative idea in your self-talk, lightly snap the elastic on your wrist. This becomes a mental "reset button" to help you refocus on the positive. The first few days of doing this might be painful, but as you become more conscious of your self-talk, you will find that you have sensitized yourself to your negative thinking and such thoughts decrease. *Don't overdo this.* The idea is to create awareness of your habits, not to punish yourself for them.

You can use your self-talk either to reinforce your goal achievement habit or to hold yourself back. Use your self-talk to focus on what you want. Ask yourself questions such as "What's the best use of my time right now?" "How can I move towards my goal right now?" "What would my role model do in this situation?" Examine your self-talk on a regular basis to make sure that your subconscious is working with you to create the future you want rather than holding you back in the past you want to leave behind. Changing it can be one of the most effective steps you can take to keep your goals top of mind and at top of your to-do list.

What To Do With Your Excess Baggage

"Baggage" is another aspect of self-talk and your subconscious. All of your past experiences leave impressions on your mind. Your previous successes and failures influence your reactions, your behaviors, your habits. Sometimes you carry forward past experiences. For example, if you have had bad experiences with the opposite sex, you might become jaded and take on an attitude that "all men are unreliable" or "all women are gossips." These preconceived ideas become baggage that is carried forward into any new relationship and will affect your behavior. How successful can any new relationship be when you try to put your baggage on the other person's shoulders?

The problem with baggage is that it is hard to see. First you must find it and then you must be prepared to put in the energy to get rid of it. Leave your baggage behind!

Leaving Your Baggage Behind

Imagine that you're at an airport. You've just arrived at your destination. You're eager to get going. Old friends and new adventures await you. You're at the baggage carousel. Impatiently, you wait and wait. The carousel finally starts. The baggage of your fellow passengers begins trundling by on the conveyor belt. Each piece has a nametag. You recognize one of your bags on the other side. You see someone reach for it. You feel apprehensive, but they put it back. What a relief!

You see, at this airport, there's a twist. Here, you can choose which bags you want to take with you—you don't have to leave with your own beat-up suitcase. When you see that old familiar Samsonite, you remember what you left in it—memories of broken relationships, past failures, pain caused by others, guilt, embarrassment, misdirection, lack of commitment.

Be happy when you see that suitcase because now you know exactly where it is. You know that your fond memories and happy moments are packed elsewhere and that you were wise enough to pack all your junk together. Now, just walk away! Leave it behind with the other unclaimed bags. Hope that it goes to the dumpster of discarded pasts or some distant asylum for lost socks and other misplaced articles. If you absolutely can't turn your back on it and must take it, hire a porter! Don't carry it yourself. You have a life to live and a future to create, unencumbered by old habits and preconceived ideas of questionable merit. Keep both hands free to grab the new and more desirable things in your life. Reach for positive values and warm relationships. Leave behind your suitcase full of past failure, fear of a broken heart, disloyalty, or disappointment.

Looking Ahead

In this chapter, you have delved deep inside several of the key components of making meaningful and achievable goals. You have identified your current values and assets, and identified the asset shortfalls that need to be overcome. You perfected both your strategic and tactical goal definitions and goal priorities so that you can focus on your greatest values. Now that you have this critically important starting point, you are ready to learn more about the Goal Achievement Process that will simplify your efforts and keep your activities on target. In the next chapter, you will tackle the skill of defining your goals so that they are clear, important to you, in writing, and most of all S.M.A.R.T. (specific, measurable, achievable, realistic, and timely).

Chapter 9
Converting Dreams Into Goals

What is a goal? By most definitions, a goal is an "end" towards which a "process" has been developed and implemented to ensure its achievement. If a goal is not an achievement target, then it cannot be completed. It becomes the process itself—without a timeline and with limited opportunity for improvement. I see the situation a little differently. For me, yes, a goal is a milestone to be achieved; however, once achieved, it becomes part of your history. There is another milestone ahead, marking the achievement of the next logical goal in the series. The Goal Achievement Process is valuable because it makes the goal achievable and it can be transferred between goals and between the stages within a greater goal. Having a consistent, tactical process helps ensure the "achievability" of the goal. The process can be observed, monitored, measured, and modified. You can *delegate or share parts of the process with others who do not need to commit to ownership of the goal.* You cannot delegate your goal. You can only delegate parts of the process.

Goals need to be put into motion—made "operational." A goal without a process to achieve it is only a dream. It is something you intend to do at some future date. It will remain such, as long as there is no committed implementation plan (process) to achieve it.

Turning Intentions Into True Goals

Often people try to turn their good intentions into goals. It does not matter whether the goal is small or big. Until these intentions are truly converted into realistic, committed goals, they remain only intentions. To make sure that your intentions become your true goals, ask yourself the following:

★ Whose goal is it?

★ Is it a goal or just a good intention?

★ Should your goal be written down?

★ How often should your review your goals?

★ What are the steps involved in achieving this goal?

Any goal you give your full commitment to becomes your goal. If you are not committed to its achievement, it is not your goal. It might be your dream or intention or even someone else's dream for you, but *it is not your goal until you take ownership and implement the process to achieve it.*

Written goals have more permanence and are more memorable than unwritten goals. They are easier to evaluate, modify, and refine. They are also easier to review on a daily basis. Written goals can be elaborated upon and expanded on to flesh out the details, to firm up the commitment and to create the Goal Achievement Process. Daily review is a major factor in the "Persistence" of the goal. Without daily recommitment and action, other priorities will replace your important goals and their processes will bog down, and eventually stagnate.

Is daily review too much? For some goals, daily review might appear to be too often. But if the goal is one of the five most important activities in your life, why wouldn't you want to focus a portion of your attention and energy on it every day? If you are not working on one of your top five priorities, then what are you working on? This gets back to our tipping point principles of focus, empowerment, and persistence. What assurance do you have that you will go back to working on them again tomorrow or the next day, or ever?

This chapter explores strategies for breaking down goals into daily bite-size pieces that will move you progressively towards their achievement. You start with small goals that work up to your big goal.

Small goals are stepping-stones on the path towards much bigger goals. As you progressively achieve small goals, you can achieve big outcomes. Big goals require extra effort. They need to be orchestrated, coordinated, timelined, and monitored. Big goals will not keep themselves automatically on schedule. Clear definition of the stages (milestones) and substages (stepping-stones) define the overall process and are critical to the goal's achievement.

A big goal must be broken down into daily steps that lead to either short-term stages or a mid-term "reach for the stars" goal that is far beyond your immediate capability. A long-range goal requires several stages to be completed along the way. For example, building a business to ten times the current sales level over the next four years might be a mid-term "reach for the stars" goal.

Linking Goals And Dreams

Building a bridge is a good example of a major goal. How did the Golden Gate Bridge get built? For that matter, how does any bridge get built?

First, someone has an idea or dream to link two locations via a bridge. (goal definition)

Second, architects draw plans, and identify cost, materials, resources, timelines. (establish needs)

Third, finances, contracts, and resources are sought and obtained. (establish resources)

Fourth, schedules and budgets are set. (plan finalized)

Fifth, specialists and general workers are employed and work is commenced with the intent to keep on budget and on schedule. (plan implemented)

Sixth, everyone celebrates the completion. (goal achieved)

So, it all starts with a dream, crystallizes through a process, and ends with a schedule achieved. Any major goal that you choose to set becomes your personal Golden Gate Bridge—a project where your future connects back to your present. (Take a moment…pause and read the last sentence again. Think about what it is telling you!)

The first step is always the hardest. This is especially true when trying to give operational-level clarity and momentum to a long-held "Someday I will…" dream-goal. If you find it a little difficult to get started, use the following twelve points as a means to ramping up towards your first Tactical Goals Achievement Process. As you read the following, you might even consider these twelve points to be the Six-Step Tactical Goals Achievement Process with training wheels.

1. Define the goal. What is the main task you want to complete?
2. Write it all down as a goal statement.
3. Evaluate the goal statement. Is it S.M.A.R.T.? Is it achievable, important, specific? Can it be completed? Is it a worthy challenge?
4. Redefine the goal statement (based on your S.M.A.R.T. evaluation in Step 2 above).
5. Envision the outcome of completion: What will it feel like? How will your five senses experience the outcome (i.e., sight, smell, sounds, touch, taste)?
6. Establish the payoff. Why will this be worthwhile? How will you benefit?
7. Set the completion date.

8. Decide on the interim stages (or milestones) and timelines. What stage can you begin (or complete) now?

9. Examine your first interim stage. Break it down into specific do-able actions.

10. Define the immediate steps needed to achieve the first interim stage and the timelines (stepping-stones).

11. Track (monitor, measure, and record) performance against the plan.

12. Once the first stage has been completed, repeat for each successive stage of the process.

Goals are more than just targets. Goals are the secret to converting a vague dream into concrete reality. As we move forward, we need a consistent approach to organizing and laying out our thought process for each goal we tackle. This tool should include a precise definition of the goal we want to achieve. It should give us insight into the obstacles that will block our progress and our strategies for overcoming them. It should lay out the scope of the project, the assets and resources needed, and the timetable required from both a macro (milestone) and a micro (stepping-stone) perspective. Once in place, this will give us the blueprint for building to our goal's completion. I call this tool the "Goal-Setting Blueprint." Introduced in Diagram 6, it will help you organize your goal information and your progress targets. I have designed this goal-setting template with three major sections (I am sure you can guess what they are):

1. **Focus:** Setting the long-term goal, including both strategic and tactical definitions.

2. **Empowerment:** Creating the mid-term milestones.

3. **Persistence:** Setting the short-term "stepping-stone" actions required to achieve the current milestone.

Here is a brief overview of the elements of Diagram 6, your Goal-Setting Blueprint. There are two sections to this format.

The first section (A) is your big-picture strategy and has three parts. The second section (B) is an inventory of the Empowerment Aids that you will need to achieve your goals.

Part 1: Focus—Setting Your Long-Term Goal. You start by focusing on your goal definition (a)—ideally on both a strategic (visionary) and tactical (implementable) level. This sets your direction. Then you go on to do (b), quality control on your goal statement: Is it S.M.A.R.T.? If it is, move forward. If not, you will need to rework it until both you and your goal are S.M.A.R.T.

In the next step (c), you picture the outcome first from a negative perspective and then a positive one. From the negative, you summarize your favorite techniques at self-sabotage—how you best engage in "sinking your own ship" with a goal of this nature. Because no one knows you better than you do, this is your opportunity to itemize your most favorite strategies for scuttling your goal achievement activities. (Come on, you know what you do best when it comes to sinking your own ship. This is your time to be truthful about how you have given in, lost faith, or given up in the past. Be honest with yourself! Your goal is to change your perspective on goal achievement, so list your best excuses here.)

Then in step (d) you picture your outcome from the positive perspective with rewards. These are the little strategies that you will implement to stay in the game and overcome your best "ship-scuttling" excuses. The objective is to keep you interested, motivated, and committed to your goal.

Next, we come to step (e), set a deadline. This is your big-picture, "let's celebrate our success" date. You will want to make sure it is a realistic date, based upon the milestones that you need to pass on the way to your goal's achievement. Pencil in your target date, but revisit it once you have completed Parts 2 and 3 below, which lay out the milestones and stepping-stones for achieving your goal.

Part 2: Empowerment, Section A—Defining Your Mid-Term Milestones. In the following step, you define your mid-term milestones. These are the major benchmarks that you want to achieve. Ideally, you would establish them based upon the progress that you want to achieve after each 90-day period. Although these milestones are all important, the most crucial is the first (or once you have achieved it, the next) one. This is the stage that is most concrete in your mind. You can perceive this stage's finish line just 90 days ahead. This stage is "operationizable." You know what you need to do and you can perceive what resources you will need to do it. Use the second (B) section of this form to define your resource requirements.

Part 3: Persistence—Keeping Short-Term Activities on Target. With your first milestone laid out—your first 90-day target—you know the next significant change you want to achieve. Use Part 3—short-term actions, or stepping-stones—to identify what you need to do and by when to achieve this next 90-day milestone. These stepping-stones are your "daily do-differentlies." They are the significant changes that you know will move you towards your milestone target. Although progressive (sequential stepping-stones are a great way to start), these stepping-stones can be independent of each other. They are the key points of your next milestone. All need to be achieved within the current 90 days—sequential or not.

Section B. This is the "expansion" of Part 2 (Empowerment), Section A. You will find plenty of room here to identify and itemize the specific tools and resources that you will need to truly empower the milestones and stepping-stones of your Goal Achievement Process. Empowerment is the "no excuses" aspect of working on a goal. You will want to make sure you have all the tools that you will need to get the job done. (You would not want a carpenter running to the hardware store for nails halfway through a job, so make sure you have what you need to complete your job here too.)

There will be a Goal-Setting Blueprint for each goal you set. You will need to revisit it regularly and to update Part 3 (Persistence) for each new 90-day milestone period. By completing the Blueprint, you will have your "reach for the stars" goal, your next four 90-day periods of milestone activities to be achieved, and the specific stepping-stone items to be accomplished over the next 90 days laid out in very precise detail. As you approach the end of each 90-day milestone period, you will need to define the steps to be taken for the next coming period.

Diagram 6A: Your Goal-Setting Blueprint

1. Setting Your Long-Term Goal	<u>Your Focus:</u> a. What do you want to achieve the most?	Strategic (Value): Tactical (Goal):
	b. Is your goal S.M.A.R.T.? –Clear –Important to me –Written down	**S.** Specific/ Concrete.........................Open-ended **M.** Measurable/ Precise ....Vague target **A.** Achievable Challenge ....Far-fetched/ Stress Inducing **R.** Realistic/ Important to me..............Marginally "interesting" to me **T.** Timely/ Able to have a deadline.....No timeline /Ongoing process
	c. Picture your outcome: "Sinking your own ship" Demotivators, Excuses	Excuse 1 Excuse 2 Excuse 3 Excuse 4
	d. Picture your outcome: "The game within the game" Motivators, Rewards	Reward 1 Reward 2 Reward 3 Reward 4
	e. Set the deadline to celebrate your success	
2. Defining Your Mid-Term Milestones	<u>Your Empowerment - A:</u> Build a timeline in 90-day increments: List this year's 90-day milestones that must be achieved for you to reach your long-term goal.(Use Table B to identify milestone empowerment needs)	Today _____ Finish by _____ 90-Day Milestone 1 by 180-Day Milestone 2 by 270-Day Milestone 3 by 365-Day Milestone 4 by
3. Keeping Short-Term Activities on Target	**Your Persistence:** Stepping-Stones: List the basic daily changes or weekly activities that will move you toward your next milestone.	Milestone No. __ Stepping-Stone Action 1 Stepping-Stone Action 2 Stepping-Stone Action 3 Stepping-Stone Action 4 Stepping-Stone Action 5

© Copyright Lou Mulligan 2009

Diagram 6B: Your Goal-Setting Blueprint - Empowerment Aids

Tactical Goal: _____ Date:_____

Milestone/Stepping-Stone	Empowerment Aids
1.	
2.	
3.	
4.	
5.	

© Copyright Lou Mulligan 2009

Why so much detail and precision? One reason is that most people seldom think beyond the current step. Consequently, they get bogged down when they get close to accomplishing the current stepping-stone target and it is time to transition to the next step. You need to think of each milestone not just as a stage but also as a major transition point. Each time you come to a transition point, you have achieved a major step that qualifies you to go on to a higher level. Think of each stepping-stone as a minor transition point. Either you achieve it or your goal achievement plan gets bogged down. These stepping-stones become important every time you encounter one of your daily bottlenecks or, when working on a priority item, you find yourself engaged in one of your best goal-scuttling excuses.

These bottlenecks also occur when your different priorities merge and your "alligator got-a-do's" come in conflict with your "swamp-draining got-a-do's." (If you had drained the swamp, you would have fewer and very tired alligators to deal with.) Most times, the alligator got-a-do's win because they assume a higher urgency. Nonetheless, this does not mean that your real priorities should be disregarded, only that they need you to refocus your vision on their critical importance to you.

This talk about alligators and swamp-draining got-a-do's may sound kind of silly, but step back for a moment and think about your life in the past week. How much time did you spend on fighting fires and problem solving? This represents the time you were beating down your personal alligators. How much time did you spend working on your top priorities? Alligators lurk in the murky swamp of conflicting priorities. They sneak up and surprise you. When this happens, you probably stop working "proactively" on your true priority and shift to "reactive" work on today's crises. Because you have gone from your top priority to your urgent priority, transitioning back will create a bottleneck when you must decide what to work on next. You might say "that never happens to me, I can stay on top of things," but every ringing telephone, every coffee refill, every bathroom break represents another opportunity to get sidetracked—a bottleneck in disguise, with a goal-disturbing alligator lurking behind it.

Management By Bottlenecks

Bottlenecks are where goal achievement processes break down. Professor Eliyahi Goldratt, the father of the Theory of Constraints, believes that you can consider every process to be like a chain. For him, any process becomes as good as its weakest link. The weakest link is where progress gets bogged down and a bottleneck develops. This will be recognizable as a transition point. When you are managing a process, you need to look for these bogged-down transition points and use your awareness of them as a means to define and streamline your goal achievement process.

For our purposes here, your bottlenecks are the points where your focus shifts and your resolve is weakened. On a micro, day-to-day basis, this could be from any interruption—a phone call, a paper jam in your printer, a coffee break—anything that takes you away from your priority and places you in a position where you need to decide what you will do next—go back to your priority or go on to a different task. On a 90-day milestone basis, this could be an influenza that sidelines you for two weeks, or a special project that your boss needs as soon as possible. Bottlenecks tell you that a process will break down wherever the transitional flow bogs down (i.e., a bottleneck) as it moves from one stage to the next. Significantly, this is exactly what happens when you undermine your Goal Achievement Process by shifting your focus from your highest priority to any alternative priority. You go through a transition and a bottleneck develops in relation to your main priority. You have shifted your focus—your goal is no longer the goal. Using Eliyahu Goldratt's insight, examine where, when, and why your goals get sidetracked. Use benchmarks (milestones and stepping-stones) to turn transitional bottlenecks into red flags. Use your awareness of your favorite ship-sinking tactics, your best "game within the game" defenses, to get back on track in advance.

The Role Played By Resolve

The strength of your goal is determined by the strength of your personal resolve to achieve it and by your ability to keep your process humming along—even when sidetracked.

The strength of your personal resolve is determined by the committed presence of the goal in your mind and actions (Persistence). Your process for keeping the goal and the next steps towards completion "top of mind" is key to your steady progress towards achieving each milestone. If your weakest link is following up, then that is where your process requires support. If your weakest link is shifting priorities, then that is where your bottleneck lies. Once you know your weakest link, you can develop strategies to turn it into an advantage.

Every day you have many priorities and commitments. Keeping your personal goals top of mind takes regular effort. Use your process to reinforce your good intentions. When you think about your goal and take action towards it, you reinforce its priority as *your* goal.

This concludes Part Three—Empowerment. Going back to the quote from Aristotle,

First, have a definite, clear practical ideal, a goal, an objective.

Second, have the necessary means to achieve your ends: wisdom, money, materials and methods.

Third adjust all your means to that end.

We have explored the issues of Focus and Empowerment. We are now ready for Part Four—Activating the Paradigm: Advanced. By the end of Part Four, you will know what your goals are and how to keep committed to them as memorable targets each and every day.

PART FOUR

Activating The Paradigm

BE PERSISTENT!

Third, adjust all your means to that end.

Chapter 10
Setting Your Goals In Dynamic Motion

In the last chapter, you were introduced to the Goal-Setting Blueprint, a very powerful tool for summarizing your thoughts and plans for each goal. Now, it is time to use the Goal-Setting Blueprint to provide structure and motion to your goals. In this chapter, you will be tying together the Strategic Goals Incubator dimension of your goals with the Tactical Goal Achievement Process, bringing them both in line with the Whole Person Concept elements for each asset area.

Once the goal is set, the Goal Achievement Process gives it life and creates a natural continuation from one stepping-stone cycle to the next as you move from implementing your recommendations to collect new data and re-evaluate how the implementation plan is working. In turn, you modify or change the plan as needed.

Here is a quick overview of this section: The five chapters in Part Four help you create your personal goal achievement programs for each of the Whole Person Concept elements. In this chapter, the focus is on taking the Goal-Setting Blueprint introduced in the last chapter and filling in the blanks. You will set up your tactical plans for each of the five Whole Person Concept goals that you have established. In the following chapter, the focus shifts to your Goal Reset Button—the best persistence strategy for staying on top of your daily priorities—and the key to the 7 "P's" of successful goal achievement. This is followed by Chapters 12 and 13, which focus on strategies to streamline your goal achievement efforts, including whether to consider hiring a qualified coach/mentor. Chapter 14 wraps this section up by discussing the importance of your habits—the ones you want to keep as well as the ones you do not.

So let's not waste another moment. There has been lots of talk and lots of description. Now it is time to roll up your sleeves and dive into your top five goals! Please refer to Chapter 8 (Exercise 16) for the goals you have been developing. You will need a realistic time horizon, an understanding of your level of commitment, and a summary of your available and required resources. I suggest that both your stepping-stone actions and mid-term milestones be designed in 90-day stages. (If necessary, please refer back to Chapter 9 for details regarding how to complete these tables.)

Physical Health Goals

Physical refers to all aspects of your bodily health, ranging from the obvious dimensions of weight, strength, and flexibility to the more esoteric, such as decreasing cholesterol levels, improving hand-eye coordination, or effectively eliminating toxins in your body.

Complete Exercise 18, The Goal-Setting Blueprint, to clarify your Physical Health goal and Goal Achievement Process. Remember to use the Goal-Setting Blueprint's Section B to identify the assets and resources that you will need to truly empower your Physical Health goal.

NOTE: The Goal-Setting Blueprint, Exercise 18, is included here, in a "non-fill-in-able" format, for your reference. Exercises 19–22, variations on this same template for the other four elements of the Whole Person Concept, appear in similar format. As mentioned in the Introduction, full-size exercise templates are available at the companion website **www.HeyIcandoThis.com**.

Exercise 18A: Goal-Setting Blueprint—Physical Health

1. Setting Your Long-Term Goal	<u>Your Focus:</u> a. What do you want to achieve the most?	Strategic (Value): Tactical (Goal):
	b. Is your goal S.M.A.R.T.? –Clear –Important to me –Written down	**S.** Specific/ Concrete.........................Open-ended **M.** Measurable/ Precise ....Vague target **A.** Achievable Challenge ....Far-fetched/ Stress Inducing **R.** Realistic/ Important to me..............Marginally "interesting" to me **T.** Timely/ Able to have a deadline.....No timeline /Ongoing process
	c. Picture your outcome: "Sinking your own ship" Demotivators, Excuses	Excuse 1 Excuse 2 Excuse 3 Excuse 4
	d. Picture your outcome: "The game within the game" Motivators, Rewards	Reward 1 Reward 2 Reward 3 Reward 4
	e. Set the deadline to celebrate your success	
2. Defining Your Mid-Term Milestones	<u>Your Empowerment - A:</u> Build a timeline in 90-day increments: List this year's 90-day milestones that must be achieved for you to reach your long-term goal.(Use Table B to identify milestone empowerment needs)	Today _____ Finish by _____ 90-Day Milestone 1 by 180-Day Milestone 2 by 270-Day Milestone 3 by 365-Day Milestone 4 by
3. Keeping Short-Term Activities on Target	Your Persistence: **Stepping-Stones:** List the basic daily changes or weekly activities that will move you toward your next milestone.	Milestone No. ___ Stepping-Stone Action 1 Stepping-Stone Action 2 Stepping-Stone Action 3 Stepping-Stone Action 4 Stepping-Stone Action 5

© Copyright Lou Mulligan 2009

Diagram 18B: Empowerment Aids

Tactical Goal: _____ Date:_____

Milestone/Stepping-Stone	Empowerment Aids
1.	
2.	
3.	
4.	
5.	

© Copyright Lou Mulligan 2009

Spiritual Health Goals

For some, Spiritual Health refers to a private, inner-focused pursuit. For others, spirituality is more closely associated with organized religious beliefs, customs, and activities. Some people may seek spirituality through science or through living an exemplary life. Using the Goal-Setting Blueprint (Exercise 19, available at **www.HeyIcandoThis.com**), clarify the goal you have been developing thus far for the Spiritual Health dimension of your life. As with your Physical Health, you need to determine your quality of life stage (strategic) and your major goal's (tactical) situation. Have a realistic time horizon, an understanding of your level of commitment (risk tolerance), and your available resources. Design your short-term stepping-stone actions and your mid-term milestones in 90-day stages.

Exercise 19A: Goal-Setting Blueprint—Spiritual Health

1. Setting Your Long-Term Goal	Your Focus: a. What do you want to achieve the most?	Strategic (Value): Tactical (Goal):
	b. Is your goal S.M.A.R.T.? –Clear –Important to me –Written down	S. Specific/ Concrete..........................Open-ended M. Measurable/ Precise ....Vague target A. Achievable Challenge ....Far-fetched/ Stress Inducing R. Realistic/ Important to me..............Marginally "interesting" to me T. Timely/ Able to have a deadline.....No timeline /Ongoing process
	c. Picture your outcome: "Sinking your own ship" Demotivators, Excuses	Excuse 1 Excuse 2 Excuse 3 Excuse 4
	d. Picture your outcome: "The game within the game" Motivators, Rewards	Reward 1 Reward 2 Reward 3 Reward 4
	e. Set the deadline to celebrate your success	
2. Defining Your Mid-Term Milestones	Your Empowerment - A: Build a timeline in 90-day increments: List this year's 90-day milestones that must be achieved for you to reach your long-term goal.(Use Table B to identify milestone empowerment needs)	Today _____ Finish by _____ 90-Day Milestone 1 by 180-Day Milestone 2 by 270-Day Milestone 3 by 365-Day Milestone 4 by
3. Keeping Short-Term Activities on Target	Your Persistence: Stepping-Stones: List the basic daily changes or weekly activities that will move you toward your next milestone.	Milestone No. ___ Stepping-Stone Action 1 Stepping-Stone Action 2 Stepping-Stone Action 3 Stepping-Stone Action 4 Stepping-Stone Action 5

© Copyright Lou Mulligan 2009

Social Health Goals

Whether you prefer lively groups or quiet isolation, you always have a social dimension to your life. Social relationships vary in their purpose, intimacy, and duration. Yet most people define many aspects of themselves based upon their perception of how others feel about them. Because relationships are constantly evolving, your ability to create and nurture the ones you need is key to your health. Your Social Health goals also include your relationships with your civic responsibilities and ecological obligations in your life. Referring back to the Social Health Goal you have decided upon, use The Goal-Setting Blueprint (Exercise 20 from **www.HeyIcandoThis.com**) to clarify and develop your Social Health goal. Remember to design your short-term stepping-stone actions and your mid-term milestones in 90-day stages.

Exercise 20A: Goal-Setting Blueprint—Social Health

1. Setting Your Long-Term Goal	Your Focus: a. What do you want to achieve the most?	Strategic (Value): Tactical (Goal):
	b. Is your goal S.M.A.R.T.? –Clear –Important to me –Written down	S. Specific/ Concrete.........................Open-ended M. Measurable/ Precise ....Vague target A. Achievable Challenge ....Far-fetched/ Stress Inducing R. Realistic/ Important to me...............Marginally "interesting" to me T. Timely/ Able to have a deadline.....No timeline /Ongoing process
	c. Picture your outcome: "Sinking your own ship" Demotivators, Excuses	Excuse 1 Excuse 2 Excuse 3 Excuse 4
	d. Picture your outcome: "The game within the game" Motivators, Rewards	Reward 1 Reward 2 Reward 3 Reward 4
	e. Set the deadline to celebrate your success	
2. Defining Your Mid-Term Milestones	Your Empowerment - A: Build a timeline in 90-day increments: List this year's 90-day milestones that must be achieved for you to reach your long-term goal.(Use Table B to identify milestone empowerment needs)	Today _____ Finish by _____ 90-Day Milestone 1 by 180-Day Milestone 2 by 270-Day Milestone 3 by 365-Day Milestone 4 by
3. Keeping Short-Term Activities on Target	Your Persistence: Stepping-Stones: List the basic daily changes or weekly activities that will move you toward your next milestone.	Milestone No. ____ Stepping-Stone Action 1 Stepping-Stone Action 2 Stepping-Stone Action 3 Stepping-Stone Action 4 Stepping-Stone Action 5

© Copyright Lou Mulligan 2009

Intellectual Health Goals

Do you interpret personal events subjectively or objectively? Are you able to use past experiences to develop situational guidelines separating your reaction from the stimulus you are responding to? Do you have a strategy or process for gathering, interpreting, and assimilating new experiences? Use The Goal-Setting Blueprint (Exercise 21 from **www.HeyIcandoThis.com**) to detail your Intellectual Health goal and the steps required to set it in motion. If you need to, please refer to Chapter 8, Exercise 16, for the goals you have been developing. Keeping your program under control is important, so remember to design your stepping-stone actions and your mid-term milestones in 90-day stages.

Exercise 21A: Goal-Setting Blueprint—Intellectual Health

1. Setting Your Long-Term Goal	Your Focus: a. What do you want to achieve the most?	Strategic (Value): Tactical (Goal):		
	b. Is your goal S.M.A.R.T.? –Clear –Important to me –Written down	S. Specific/ Concrete..........................Open-ended M. Measurable/ Precise ....Vague target A. Achievable Challenge ....Far-fetched/ Stress Inducing R. Realistic/ Important to me..............Marginally "interesting" to me T. Timely/ Able to have a deadline.....No timeline /Ongoing process		
	c. Picture your outcome: "Sinking your own ship" Demotivators, Excuses	Excuse 1 Excuse 2 Excuse 3 Excuse 4		
	d. Picture your outcome: "The game within the game" Motivators, Rewards	Reward 1 Reward 2 Reward 3 Reward 4		
	e. Set the deadline to celebrate your success			
2. Defining Your Mid-Term Milestones	Your Empowerment - A: Build a timeline in 90-day increments: List this year's 90-day milestones that must be achieved for you to reach your long-term goal.(Use Table B to identify milestone empowerment needs)	Today _____ Finish by _____ 90-Day Milestone 1 by 180-Day Milestone 2 by 270-Day Milestone 3 by 365-Day Milestone 4 by		
3. Keeping Short-Term Activities on Target	Your Persistence: Stepping-Stones: List the basic daily changes or weekly activities that will move you toward your next milestone.	Milestone No. ___ Stepping-Stone Action 1 Stepping-Stone Action 2 Stepping-Stone Action 3 Stepping-Stone Action 4 Stepping-Stone Action 5		

© Copyright Lou Mulligan 2009

The Financial Health Goals

As you develop your financial goal further, you need to determine the status of your lifetime values (strategic) and your major goals (tactical) in relation to your financial goals.

Continue on to The Goal-Setting Blueprint (Exercise 22 from **www.HeyIcandoThis.com**). Here you will consolidate all the information into one single financial goal process. It becomes your template for your goal's achievement. Use it to pull all your thoughts together on your goal for Financial Health. Financial Health goals can range from debt reduction and investing wisely to receiving a higher level of compensation for the "value added" that you provide. Please refer to Chapter 8, Exercise 16, for the goals you have been developing. Take advantage of the structure provided by the 90-Day Follow-Up Strategy. (The 90-Day Follow-Up Strategy will be detailed in Chapter 12.) Design your goal achievement targets such that every 90 days you will have reached the next stage of your goal achievement program.

Exercise 22A: Goal-Setting Blueprint—Financial Health

1. Setting Your Long-Term Goal	<u>Your Focus:</u> **a. What do you want to achieve the most?**	Strategic (Value): Tactical (Goal):
	b. Is your goal S.M.A.R.T.? –Clear –Important to me –Written down	**S.** Specific/ Concrete..........................Open-ended **M.** Measurable/ Precise ....Vague target **A.** Achievable Challenge ....Far-fetched/ Stress Inducing **R.** Realistic/ Important to me...............Marginally "interesting" to me **T.** Timely/ Able to have a deadline.....No timeline /Ongoing process
	c. Picture your outcome: **"Sinking your own ship"** **Demotivators, Excuses**	Excuse 1 Excuse 2 Excuse 3 Excuse 4
	d. Picture your outcome: **"The game within the game"** **Motivators, Rewards**	Reward 1 Reward 2 Reward 3 Reward 4
	e. Set the deadline to celebrate your success	
2. Defining Your Mid-Term Milestones	<u>Your Empowerment - A:</u> **Build a timeline in 90-day increments:** List this year's 90-day milestones that must be achieved for you to reach your long-term goal.(Use Table B to identify milestone empowerment needs)	Today _____ Finish by _____ 90-Day Milestone 1 by 180-Day Milestone 2 by 270-Day Milestone 3 by 365-Day Milestone 4 by
3. Keeping Short-Term Activities on Target	**Your Persistence:** **Stepping-Stones:** List the basic daily changes or weekly activities that will move you toward your next milestone.	Milestone No. ___ Stepping-Stone Action 1 Stepping-Stone Action 2 Stepping-Stone Action 3 Stepping-Stone Action 4 Stepping-Stone Action 5

© Copyright Lou Mulligan 2009

There, you have done it! Congratulations! You have established your top five goals within the Living on Purpose Paradigm. You have defined what needs to be done over the next 13 weeks. You have set the Major Goal Momentum stages for each of your five goals at the starting line.

One of the first things that you will run up against is the inevitable conflict between what you should do and the day-to-day reality of what you must do. The next chapter will help you develop strategies to keep you on target and make it easier to stay on track and difficult for you to get detoured through some alligator-infested swamp.

Remember, this race is a marathon, not a sprint. Now you just have to do it—one day at a time.

Chapter 11
Stepping-Stones To Moving Forward

*Everyday as soon as you get up, you can develop a sincere positive
motivation, thinking, "I will utilize this day in a more positive way. I
should not waste this very day.' And then, at night before you go to
bed, check what you have done, asking yourself, "Did I utilize this
day as I planned?" If it went accordingly, you should rejoice! If it
went wrong, then regret what you did and critique the day. So,
through methods such as this, you can gradually strengthen the
positive aspects in your mind.*

—The Dalai Lama[5]

Your goals are in place. You have set your 90-day milestones
and the progressive stepping-stones to move you forward. Notice
how much clearer you are about your priorities and what you are
willing to do. You are focused and feel empowered. But, despite
this organizational effort, you might still encounter difficulty in
achieving your goals.

Although you have spent a great deal of time developing your
goals, you can still get sidetracked and spend all your time on
urgencies rather than priorities. Chapter 1 introduced the idea of
the Priority Reset Button that helps you get back to your true priorities. Exercise 23 serves this purpose. Use this format to keep
your daily goal stepping-stone activities on target. Use it to structure a new time habit where you set aside time to refresh and

[5] His Holiness The Dalai Lama and Howard C. Cutler, M.D., *The Art of
Happiness, A Handbook For Living*. New York: Riverhead Books, a member of
Penguin Putnam, Inc., 1998, p. 42.

re-invigorate your goals focus. Let this become your personal priority oasis—time set aside for your game plan, time where you "prioritize your priorities," and time to review your progress at day's end.

You will be amazed at how simple yet effective this Priority Reset Button can be! Take a look, then read the legend that follows.

Exercise 23: The Priority Reset Button

Today's Primary Objectives-Whole Person Concept					
Name:			Date:		
(1) PRIOR-ITY	(2) Today I Will... (Focus)	(3) Key Question (Persistence)	(4) Best Progress (Empowerment Level 1)	(5) Okay Progress (Empowerment Level 2)	(6) Today's Actual Result
	Physical Health (example)	How can I reinforce my new diet habit today?	Eat a salad with lunch and dinner.	Do not add sugar to anything.	2 black coffees—YUK! I'm switching to water tomorrow!! 1 salad = progress
	Physical Health				
	Spiritual Health				
	Social Health				
	Intellectual Health				
	Financial Health				
	Wild Card Priority 1				
	Wild Card Priority 2				

© 2005 Lou Mulligan.

Copies of the Priority Reset Button are available at www.HeyIcandoThis.com.

After hearing the following story about Charles M. Schwab when he was president of Bethlehem Steel, I was motivated to develop the Priority Reset Button (Exercise 23) format. Here is the story....

Genesis Of This Format

In the early 1900s, Schwab wanted to increase the efficiency of his management team at Bethlehem Steel as well as his own personal effectiveness. Ivy Lee, a management consultant who later became one of the fathers of public relations, gave Schwab a 3 × 5 card and said, "Take this card and list the six most important tasks you have to do tomorrow on it. Number them in their order of importance. Put the card in your pocket and first thing tomorrow morning, look at Item 1 and start working on it. Pull the card out every 15 minutes and read Item 1 until it's finished. Then tackle Item 2 in the same way, and then Item 3. Keep doing this until quitting time. Don't be concerned if you only finish one or two items during the day. You'll be working on the most important one first. The others can wait. Spend the last 5 minutes of every day making out your 'must-do list' for the next day."

Apparently Schwab paid Lee $35,000 for the advice. (At that time, the average income of a family of five in Chicago was about $750 per year.) You can see the value that Schwab placed in this process. I thought this was a fascinating story worth serious consideration. I developed the Priority Reset Button to give structure to this idea. Many of my clients have found that this helps them keep focused upon their top priority's next actions, in spite of interruptions in their daily activities.

To use the Priority Reset Button, simply do the following:

Starting with each of your 5 Whole Person Goals (Column

2), identify the stepping-stone stage that you are working on today (Column 3). Using Columns 4 and 5, decide upon just exactly what you want to accomplish. Establish what you would consider as superior performance (Level 1) and as adequate performance (Level 2). Once you have your list complete, use Column 1 to set your priorities according to the importance to you for that day. At the end of the day, review what you actually did against your Level 1/Level 2 targets (Column 6). With your new knowledge based upon today's achievements, create your new page for tomorrow.

In regard to the Priority Reset Button, my recommendation is to start the habit of setting aside a short period of time at the start and end of each day. Five or ten minutes should be more than adequate. With your completed Goal-Setting Blueprints from Chapter 10 in hand, use this time to integrate your goals' stepping-stones into your daily plan. During the day, review your Priority Reset Button and ask yourself, "What is the best use of my time right now?"

At the end of each day, review the day's goals and ask yourself, "What did I do today that moved me closer to my goals?" Build your "must-do" list for the next morning by answering the following question: "What am I going to do tomorrow that will move me closer to each of my goals?" Once again, refer to your Goal-Setting Blueprints for each of your five Whole Person Category Goals from Chapter 10 to stay consistent and focused on the next short-term action for each of your five goals. Write down tomorrow's Priority Reset Button action plan and keep it where you can note their priority during the day. I have added "wild card" categories just in case the "alligators are overrunning your personal swamp."

Adopt an adage similar to "an apple a day keeps the doctor away"—perhaps "a goal review each night keeps my targets in sight." This makes a great Priority Reset Button. Print it out and keep it where you will refer to it often throughout the day.

At first, the idea of listing and reviewing today's top actions for your top five goals seems old-fashioned. It is definitely low tech. Well, in his day, Charles Schwab was one of the most successful businessmen in the United States. Any idea that helped him to stay focused, keep his goals in mind, and stay empowered and on track should be worth considering—even if it is old-fashioned.

The Seven P's Of Successful Goal Achievement

Your Priority Reset Button serves a very important purpose. Unless you keep your top priorities in front of you, you will end up completing someone else's priorities instead. Consider my Seven P's of Success and how this simple strategy will help you become a successful goal achiever:

★ Perfectionism

★ Procrastination

★ Platitudes

★ Perseverance

★ Purpose

★ Prominence

★ Priority

Three of these can hurt you; four will help you.

The Three "Bad" P's

Perfectionism is the quest to *never finish* what you start—because every time you get to the 95% complete or perfect level, you realize you are only halfway there. (Imagine that the novel *War and Peace*—which tilts the scales at approximately 1450 pages long—was once a short story.) Perfectionism takes the best of intentions and stretches them out so far that you never finish—and never get credit for your efforts.

By using this simple Priority Reset Button form for your daily goal review, you will be more focused and encouraged to adopt my "Good-Enough Principle." The Good-Enough Principle states that, in any endeavor, there comes a point when continued effort will only produce a marginal enhancement in results. This is the point that defines perfectionists and cripples their value to society. So, to escape from perfectionism, you must decide that 90% or 95% perfect is simply *good enough*.

Procrastination is the art of doing something else. When you procrastinate, you actively take steps to inhibit any effort at working towards your stated critical goals. When procrastination sets in, your actual goal (by default) becomes *not* achieving those critical goals that you say are important to you. Success at procrastination is failure in goal achievement. (Sound confusing? Read this again and it will begin to make sense.)

What will jump-start a procrastinator? Using the Priority Reset Button form can trick you into success. Consider what I have named "The Worthmore Initiative"—that is, people get paid for what they do—not what they know. Through The Worthmore Initiative, procrastinators and perfectionists are able to use the Priority Reset Button form to convert their knowledge-based resourcefulness into application-driven usefulness for greater contribution and added value. Simply put, you realize that your contribution will make a difference *and* that the fruits of your labor and your contribution are definitely "worth more" than you have been given credit for.

Platitudes are used when you tell yourself it is okay to give your goals low priority. You are feeding yourself platitudes in the guise of self-talk: "I'll do it later." "It's not that important anyway." "One more little one won't hurt." You might also hear platitudes from others. Do not believe everything you hear from them, even though the platitudes that others tell you are minor in relation to those that you tell yourself. While other people's platitudes can give you comfort and excuses, only you can convince yourself they are true. Worse yet is the self-talk that slips beneath your conscious mind and fools you into accepting the status quo when you could be reaching for new levels of achievement. Using the Priority Reset Button form helps you overcome platitudes because you can see them for what they really are. Think of it like the old World War II anti-espionage slogan "Loose lips can sink ships"—your platitudes are a form of self-sabotage. Platitudes can scuttle your best goal-setting efforts! Your Priority Reset Button will pull back to your true objective.

The Four "Good" P's

Perseverance brings you closer to achieving your goals more than anything else will. Perseverance wears down resistance and creates the character needed to live your life on purpose. Having a sense of purpose and going steadily towards your goals is key to achieving your dreams.

The difficulty in being perseverant lies in being able to continually keep the topic of your perseverance at the top of your mind. Without remembering why and what you are being perseverant about, it is easy to get in the habit of blindly pushing towards your goals. Although you may think you are experiencing success, you may be fooling yourself. Even perseverance needs tempering with the Priority Reset Button form's daily reality check. When used within the framework of The 90-Day Follow-Up Strategy (see Chapter 12), you will demonstrate purposeful perseverance where other programs fall short.

Purpose is why you do what you do. What is your apparent purpose? What is your *real* purpose? Know yourself and freely accept why you do the things you do without judgment. This is the first step towards living with purpose. The Priority Reset Button form helps keep your purpose foremost in your mind and in your activities.

Prominence is keeping your goals front and center in your mind at all times. It is the key to making sure you are working on your most important goals. Giving prominence to your priorities helps you remember what is important and stay focused on the areas that will lead to your greatest achievement. Keeping important ideas prominent in your mind helps you remember where you want to go and what you want to do. The Major Goals Momentum System (see Chapter 12) helps keep your major goals top of mind through the daily application of the Priority Reset Button form's structure.

Priority, by definition, is whatever you are doing—regardless of its perceived value—that is, whatever you are doing automatically becomes your "highest priority." The task, then, is to make sure there is congruency between your perceived priorities and your "actual" priorities. Work on what is truly important to you. How better to do this than by planning and reviewing your activities of today and tomorrow using the Priority Reset Button form? When you know your priorities and you have a sense of purpose, you will find it easier to keep them prominent in your mind. By consistently and perseveringly working towards your goals, you will overcome procrastination. Not letting the platitudes get to you makes it easier to move towards your goal. Knowing what you want to achieve keeps your sense of accomplishment in mind, and accepting what is good enough helps you maintain your momentum.

The next step: making your dreams happen. Chapters 12 and 13 shift focus from values, assets, and goals to you as either your own coach or a client to a coach of your choosing.

Chapter 12
Are You Ready To Make
Your Dreams Happen?

Working With Your Goals

Once you have decided upon your exact goal and established the scope of the activity, you need a procedure for working with your goals. Taking the information above, get started by using the Six-Step Tactical Goals Achievement Process below. Now, you might say, *"Here we go again...I'm sure that I've read this before...."* You're right! But before you go on, take a deep breath and consider the following. Goal setting is not rocket science, but is based upon the relationship between the top 10 New Year's Resolutions—namely,

1. Improve family relations (social)

2. Lose weight (physical)

3. Get more physically fit (physical)

4. Quit smoking (physical)

5. Quit drinking (physical)

6. Change relationships (social)

7. Get organized (intellectual)

8. Get out of debt (financial)

9. Save money (financial)

10. Enjoy life more (spiritual)

—and their successful accomplishment. If you look at the statistics on how many people actually keep to their New Year's Resolution, you might think achieving one's goals *is* more complicated than rocket science! (And notice how the top 10 resolutions tie neatly into the Whole Person Concept's five categories.)

The basic objective of the Tactical Goal Achievement Process is to develop a consistent way to approach any goal that you might ever have. Once you have it figured out, you can use the same approach for every goal. With this system, you can learn from your past experience and transfer it to ensure your future success. So, take a moment. Savor the critical importance of its simplicity. Let it sink in one more time…perhaps to a deeper subliminal level.…

The Six-Step Tactical Goal Achievement Process

1. **Define:** Write out your goal specification.

2. **Collect Data:** Take inventory to establish your current position.

3. **Assess:** Evaluate your current status regarding your goal—the difference between where you are and where you want to be.

4. **Plan/Recommend:** Decide and establish your plan of action and your progress targets and write it down.

5. **Implement:** Take action and implement your plan's recommendations.

Do this for 90 days and then…

6. **Review:** Go back and reset your goal specification. (Step 1).

Once you have mastered the understanding of this simple six-step process, it is yours for life. In the future, whenever you use this process, you will always be able to garner more wisdom from each and every one of your personal experiences. There is as much insightful wisdom in this proactive approach—an approach that you can control—than in any recent best-selling book about the secrets of the law of attraction.

Can you implement this six-step tactical process without a coach/advisor? Of course you can! *Will* you do this by yourself? I hope you do, but as indicated earlier, many people encounter difficulty when it comes to the regular follow-up dimension. That is why I have developed the Priority Reset Button and the Goals Achievement Blueprint. At a basic level, giving goals the priority that they deserve can be tricky. Like a wayward boxcar, your persistence can get sent off on some remote sidetrack—never to be seen again—at least not until a quiet moment several weeks in the future, when you suddenly say, "Oh Ya!" This is why I recommend scheduling "priority oasis time" for the regular reassessment of your progress and your re-commitment towards your goal. It is only through your persistent and committed return and reassessment of your progress towards your 90-day goal that you will keep it top of mind. Your goal's success will be more likely when you regularly revisit your goal and raise the bar every 90 days. Scheduling a review time with yourself or having to meet with your coach/advisor can help keep you on track. Of course, monitoring your performance towards your goal ultimately remains your responsibility. You need to keep ownership of it. It is your future.

Up to this point, we have placed a great deal of emphasis on the three factors of Focus, Empowerment, and Persistence. Now it is time to add two more factors critical to goal success tied to your 90-day follow-up: Momentum and Accountability.

The Major Goals Momentum And The 90-Day Follow-Up Strategy

Setting meaningful goals gives you the incentive to move forward. Creating appropriate goal achievement processes and follow-up strategies gives you the momentum.

Think of your efforts at goal achievement as part of an old cartoon set in the middle of the 19th-century gold rush in California. Imagine there are two old bewhiskered prospectors trying to "motivate" a pair of stubborn overloaded donkeys (a.k.a. your goal achievement efforts). The donkeys refuse to budge. One man in the front pulls to no avail. The other in the back pushes without success. No matter how hard they try, the donkeys (their goal) keeps resisting. Digging in their heels, the donkeys just sit there, braying—until someone comes along with a bunch of carrots, and magically, all the hee-hawing stops and the donkeys move forward towards the carrots. Well, obviously, the one with the carrots has a grander perspective or specialized knowledge and the two struggling miners obviously needed more than just pushing and pulling to get their "a_ _es" moving. And so do you. You need the added insight of a system with accountability and momentum.

The Whole Person Concept's Goal Achievement Process that you are developing is designed to start by focusing upon a strong goal and then giving it momentum. Adding the accountability of regular progress measurement every 90 days kick starts your efforts towards a higher level. This combination of momentum and accountability will launch you forward, "turbocharging" your goal achievement efforts. I describe these two forces as the "Pull" of Major Goals Momentum and the "Push" of The 90-Day Follow-Up Strategy. Here is how I developed the basics of the idea.

Imagine a figure eight...two circles, rotating, barely touching each other. The bottom one is slightly larger than the top, separate yet interconnected.

Follow the motion of the line with your eye. Start at the top. See it move clockwise, from the right side, down to the center touch point, then notice see how it crosses over and continues, counterclockwise, to the left side of the larger circle at the bottom. It moves to the lowest point, then swings back up and around to center. Follow as it moves clockwise to the top of the upper circle, then over and down towards the center, starting the figure-eight pattern once again. Follow it again. Faster. Faster. Listen closely. You can almost hear the motion of the line beginning to hum as it flows smoothly and quickly. Fluidly, no longer two circles, it changes to a never-ending belt flowing in constant motion with effortless efficiency and harmony.

Now, imagine that inside each loop of the belt, there is a wheel...spinning from the friction created by the moving belt. The top wheel spins clockwise, the bottom wheel counterclockwise. Never moving closer. Never moving farther apart. Just spinning within the belt. Spinning...an engine...a dynamo...driving energy...creating power...feeding on itself in perpetual motion. The belt pulls one wheel while pushing the other. The wheels pull the belt, yet are pushed by it at the same time. They dance and hum in a constant harmonious motion of give-and-take.

This "figure eight in motion" came to me as a "vision." But what did it mean? What was the message of the dynamo's never-ending dance of efficiency and motion?

I broke it down into elements. A belt—moving, never-ending, one side pushing, the other pulling, and two wheels linked within the loops of the belt. I knew this was important and something to be shared. My goal was to understand the symbolism and develop my vision into a useful message for all. Understanding and explaining it became my purpose.

Gradually, my vision of figure eights crystallized in my mind as a feedback system: the pushing forward of one wheel while pulling the other at the same time. But what was pushing and pulling? What was the significance of the wheels? How did it relate to my goal? What value did it hold? How did it tie into my life? Why did it obsess me?

What if it related to my goals and values? What if it meant turning my vision into a sense of motion, constantly energizing, constantly improving? Perhaps the smaller wheel represented my values and dreams, assets and values. The larger wheel represented the tools available to me to achieve my dreams and live according to my values. The never-ending belt represented the use of available tools to enhance my values and live according to my dreams. The figure-eight belt came to represent The Major Goals Momentum System pulling and The 90-Day Follow-Up Strategy pushing you towards your goal achievement success. The smaller wheel is The Goals Incubator and the larger wheel is The Six-Step Tactical Goals Achievement Process.

The Pull: The Major Goal Momentum System. Once your goal has been established, this system keeps you aware of your goal stages and tools needed. Through the Priority Reset Button and Your Goal-Setting Blueprint, the Major Goal Momentum System includes the stepping-stones and milestones that will move you from your present status to your desired life. This system puts into place focal points and benchmarks that progressively raise the bar and move you towards your goal's achievement.

The Push: The 90-Day Follow-Up Strategy. This creates the accountability of the "dynamo effect" that drives progress forward. This accountability system keeps you on track towards achieving your goals through monitoring, measuring, timekeeping, and reporting. The 90-Day Follow-Up Strategy keeps you on track towards achieving your goals.

Taken together, the interaction of "The Pull" and "The Push" forms a never-ending belt, which links your Tactical Goal Achievement Process with your Strategic Goals Incubator and moves you towards successful goal attainment. These two factors keep you on track by logging "what to do" and "what got done" as you progress.

Diagram 7 illustrates "The Pull" and "The Push" dimensions

of The Major Goals Momentum System and The 90-Day Follow-Up Strategy giving purpose, definition, urgency, and accountability to your goal achievement efforts.

Diagram 7:

The Missing Elements—Accountability And Momentum

When you have major goals that you are working towards, they create momentum in your life. When you have a strategy and a timetable, a sense of urgency is instilled. This momentum takes on a life of its own, driving your Tactical Goal Achievement Process and pulling you forward. The Major Goal Momentum System structures your activities relative to your goals by progressively raising the bar.

Complementing the "pull" dimension of the Major Goals Momentum System is the "push" dimension brought about by the need to measure progress—to create accountability. Many goal achievement programs fail at this level because of the lack of accountability. But to whom are you accountable? From the outside, you may feel that you are accountable to yourself or your coach. In reality, this person is just a detail. Your true accountability is to the goal and the progressive benchmarks that you have set. Either you achieve them or you do not. At this point, it becomes pretty black and white.

The 90-Day Follow-Up Strategy was introduced earlier. 90-day intervals give you time to accomplish something between reviews. It is neither so close that you cannot see progress, nor so far away that you lose sight of it. We are comfortable with the idea of dividing our years up quarterly into the four seasons, so using The 90-Day Follow-Up Strategy to timetable your progress will be quite natural.

Through The Pull of the Major Goals Momentum System and The Push of The 90-Day Follow-Up Strategy (as depicted in Diagram 7 above), your Goal Achievement Process becomes truly turbocharged!

Chapter 13
To Be Coached Or Not To Be Coached...That Is The Question

Goals do not automatically achieve themselves. It is your persistence in returning to the project (The 90-Day Follow-Up Strategy) and progressively moving it forward—raising the bar along the way (Major Goals Momentum System)—that sees it through to completion. Progressive goal achievement requires working towards raising targets. Even the greatest commitment and persistent application of your best intentions may still need help. For some, this help comes from measuring progress against an ideal; for others, it comes from holding themselves accountable for their progress. But how often? To whom? Whether it is "with yourself" or with someone else, you need the discipline of holding regular accountability meetings to measure your progress and set your objectives for the next period.

Tracking is important. When my children were growing up, my youngest son always wanted to be as tall as his older brothers. Being competitive, when he looked at his brothers, he was disappointed that he was shorter. Like many families, we had the tradition of marking the children's heights and ages on the kitchen door jamb. We showed him how tall his brothers had been at his age. When he saw that he was just as tall as they were at his age, he felt better, but still wanted to be taller. True to form, he is no longer the shortest. He just needed a paradigm shift to understand the situation from a different point of view.

The five Whole Person Category milestone targets you set in Chapter 10 using the Goal-Setting Blueprints give you your 90-day targets. (That is one time frame.) The Priority Reset Button introduced in Chapter 11 is designed to help you keep on track. (That is your second time frame.) Both are important. Quarterly targets set the track. Daily monitoring of your stepping-stone targets keeps you on target. Some people are able to consistently adopt The 90-Day Follow-Up Strategy on their own. Others find it easier to meet periodically with a coach.

This chapter and the next provide guidelines for either acting as your own coach or using a subject matter expert. You may not realize it, but you always have a coach. Whether you hire someone to give you guidance or not, there is always that little voice that only you can hear. It can either inspire you to superior performance or bury you in guilt. Because we are thinking positively here, we will focus on the "inspires you" side of the equation. Always program your self-talk for positive self-development.

From the Whole Person Concept's perspective of Physical, Spiritual, Social, Intellectual, and Financial Health, you have set some very significant goals. In doing so, you have given yourself a great deal of ground to cover and a significant potential need for subject matter expertise. I hope the guidelines earlier in this book will help you get your goals in motion. There might be times when you will need someone else's input and times when you will not. Personally, I believe it is better to selectively seek qualified advice to accomplish many of your goals and to move on to the next level. The alternative would be to progress at a slower pace, or to get bogged down by insisting on doing everything 100% yourself. Think about the different types of support that you might need and the duties that you might call upon a coach to provide, such as visionary guidance, subject matter expertise, or mentorship. You already have personal capability in many of these areas. For some areas and goals, you might only need selective help.

Being a "rugged individualist," doing everything by yourself, while an admirable American tradition, does not mean that you will always make progress either efficiently or effectively. Throughout this book, my goal has been to help you step back and establish perspective—to understand what you can do on your own and where you might benefit from others' expertise.

Look back at Aristotle's three principles (1) Focus, (2) Empowerment, and (3) Persistence. When it comes to 1-(Focus), developing goals that are meaningful, measurable, and achievable, and 3-(Persistence), performing the steps that make the most effective route achievable—these are obviously individual acts—either the goal setter does it or it does not get done. As regards Focus and Persistence, the coach's role is limited. However, 2-(Empowerment)—identifying the fastest route to achieving the next stage in that goal's evolution—may require new knowledge outside the goal setter's experience. Empowerment has three dimensions:

(a) The visionary "how do I achieve this goal?" You may or may not always need help with setting appropriate targets and timetables.

(b) The specialized techniques and mechanics of goal achievement. You may need help with adapting techniques, mechanics, and the success paradigm mind-set, and in deciding upon what to do differently, do next, or when to change.

(c) The accountability "what are my targets and how am I progressing against my stepping-stone targets?" You would think that most people should be able to do this on their own—after all, if you can count to 10, you should be able to record and track your performance against a pre-set target—and then just meet periodically to assess your progress.

For best results, the empowerment dimension—bringing in the coach's specialized knowledge of mechanics and techniques—will yield the best results. Unfortunately, when hiring a coach, some people may end up paying more for companionship than for the value-added wisdom. It is important to know what help you need and to contract for results as well as process. This is why we formulated and are recommending The 90-Day Follow-Up Strategy.

At a high level, The 90-Day Follow-Up Strategy creates a feedback loop. This feedback loop reinforces the goal and moves you towards its next stepping-stones and milestone. This feedback loop comes from the reality check of your 90-Day Follow-Up Strategy—the "you are here arrow" on the directory map of life. This feedback loop has two levels: (a) the long-term 90-Day Follow-Up to track the milestones and (b) the daily Priority Reset Button follow-up to track the stepping-stones. Over time, there must be a progressive change in perspective—a paradigm shift in thinking—to take the goal setter from a "wannabe" to a "bar raiser." The 90-day reviews help you recognize your progress towards your new paradigm.

This paradigm shift is important. Without it, nothing changes. Your personal balance scale will revert to its original settings—and so would you! This paradigm shift is the re-leveling factor where you change your rules, making former standards of acceptability no longer tolerable, and you tip the table in your favor. (We introduced this re-leveling idea in Chapter 8.) Your new paradigm establishes your new way of thinking. Your former balance/tipping point of what was okay is permanently shifted and no longer acceptable. You have changed. To ensure your continued success, old performance standards must change too. They must become no longer even marginally acceptable. The *new you* requires new higher standards. The feedback loop brings progressive improvement, progress measurement, and accountability.

When you do this, you are taking a fresh look at the dynamic, ever-changing relationship among (A) the progressively evolving goal outcome that you seek to achieve, (B) you, the goals setter/goals reviser, and (C) the "coach" accountability/ progress-monitoring dimensions. Productivity requires a balance among all three. (See Diagram 8.) Let's briefly discuss each of these.

Diagram 8: ABC's Of Goal Achievement

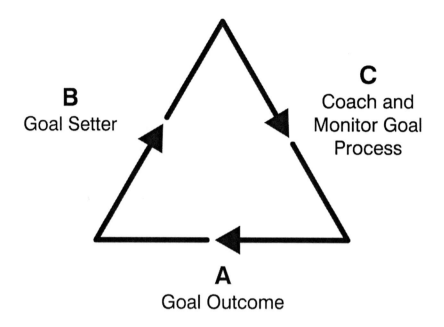

B
Goal Setter

C
Coach and
Monitor Goal
Process

A
Goal Outcome

A. Goal Outcome

We have already discussed this at great length. We stated that an ideal goal is one that you can call your own. It is not a half-hearted wish or created under someone else's influence.

Step back and look at yourself in relation to your five goals to determine your true position relative to each goal you are setting. After all, you only want to set goals that lead to your desired outcomes.

B. Goal Setter

As the goal setter, how committed are you to achieving each of your stated goals? Can you classify each goal as ideal? Do you say "I will achieve it," or "I ought to do it," or "Someday I might do it?" If "it" is an "I will" goal, then the goal's outcome and its perceived value to you are highly congruent. The goal comes with an intuitive desire to achieve it and fits like a glove. Working towards this goal will be a pleasure. If "it" is an "ought to" or "someday I might…." goal, your commitment is less than unwavering.

To keep things simple, if you cannot say that your goal is "ideal"—*then don't go there*. It is not your goal. Your potential success is in danger! Make sure you only set goals that you truly believe in.

Can you say that you are an ideal goal setter for this goal? Ideal goal setters have something they want to achieve. They are willing to allocate the resources and energy needed. They are ready to commit to taking the steps necessary to reach the desired end—no matter what obstacles slow them down. If you feel this way about your goal, then you are ready to move forward towards your dream. If you do not feel this way, it is not the end of the world. It just means that you need to re-examine your motivation until you can establish the level of commitment required for success. Being the goal setter is not drudgery. Your commitment comes from your passion. In turn, it becomes the source of your enthusiasm and your enjoyment of working at a goal that truly give you pleasure and satisfaction.

C. Coach/Advisor And Progress Monitoring

As the goal setter, you bring enthusiasm and effort to your goal achievement project. Progressive goal achievement moves you towards a higher level—a new target. Achievement targets come from the person fulfilling the role of "coach"—whether it is yourself or someone else. The coach sets the stage—establishing the mechanics, the achievement targets, and the tracking tools for monitoring progress. You need to monitor and report your performance to your coach. Structuring this around periodic 90-day reviews will save you both time and money. When you need someone to bring you a different perspective or subject matter expertise, ask yourself, "What kind of help do I need to achieve this goal? Are there any special skills that I will need and cannot supply?" The main reason for bringing in a coach should be to expand your resources so you can accelerate your success.

For simplicity, I am using *coach, consultant, mentor, advisor,* and the like interchangeably. These terms all describe someone with specialized knowledge and perspective. Many specialties require years of training and practice. Achieving certification and maintaining credentials in many specialties requires ongoing refresher courses. All their study and training makes them subject matter experts who can help you progress towards your goal. "Subject matter experts?" Yes, doctor, lawyer, certified financial planner, minister, psychologist, and in countless other professions—every accredited specialist is a subject matter expert in his or her field of knowledge. These people are here to help you. Sometimes you need them; sometimes you do not. What is important is for you to know when you do and to be committed enough to your goal's achievement to take advantage of the available expertise.

Over time, your goal achievement success may move you beyond your initial coach's capability. Through regular review, you will be able to recognize this and be prepared to move on.

If your level of commitment to your "ideal" goal is "10 out of 10," *and* you have sufficient subject matter expertise in the goal area (or can gain it quickly), then you might consider being your own "do-it-yourself" coach. However, if your commitment is not 100%, or if your expertise is lacking, you could benefit greatly from turning to a qualified, experienced coach for motivation, encouragement, perspective, and wisdom. Less than complete congruency equals less than complete results. *Don't go there.*

Why is the relationship between the goal and the goal monitoring aspect of coaching important? Setting progressive daily stepping-stone targets is critical for progress. You want these guidelines to track your progress so that you will get to where you want to go. Because your progress will normally occur gradually, daily monitoring and quarterly reviewing should be adequate in most situations. (However, if your goal is to become a professional athlete, there will be stages where your coach's daily focus on the mechanics and techniques of his or her expertise will remain necessary.) For less critical, but equally important-to-you goals such as to see more of your belt and less of your belly, having a personal trainer show up at 6:00 AM to tell you to "do just one more" may be money misspent. Although your coach does not need to take ownership of your goal, it is important that he or she adds value and perspective to your Goal Achievement Process.

If your coach is a certified professional, committed to his specialty and to your success, you are ready to move forward. However, if your coach is a friend who has been exercising two years longer than you have and would rather go out for a cold pint than push for your next level of physical perfection, reconsider this relationship. Your success depends on the coach's perspective and understanding.

In short, when you see the need for a coach, your ideal coach/advisor would be someone who is an expert in the subject matter with the appropriate credentials, experience, and perspective; someone you can relate to easily (good chemistry); someone whose fees you can afford; someone who is available on your schedule; and so on.

At some point, you might choose to settle for an "almost ideal" advisor. Perhaps you cannot find the perfect relationship match but sense certain qualities that give you sufficient comfort to go on—or perhaps the level of expertise you are seeking is not available at your current level of preparedness. Although there might be room for a more exact fit, you know where the discrepancies are. That you have established the "ideal advisor" benchmark makes you that much more committed (and that much more likely) to achieve your goal—even when you must settle for a less than perfect match.

Finding The Right Coach/Advisor

Think of yourself on the journey towards your goal like being the captain of the S.S. *Mississippi Belle*—an old paddle wheeler going up the Missouri River. You can tell just by the name that you are on the wrong river! You know your ship, you know your crew, but you do not know the river.

Today, the river is shallower than you would like, and you know that other ships have been caught on sandbars, submerged tree branches, and jagged rocks. What do you do?

★ Go bravely up the river, risking the ship, the crew, and the passengers? (Not too smart. You will need a new job soon!)

★ Get a detailed map of the river? Good! (Use technology.)

★ Go slow and position a trusted mate at the bow to watch for obstacles? Better! (Use a buddy system with vested interest.)

★ Hire the local river pilot to guide you past the dangers? Best! (Use specialized expertise.)

Just as in the example above, your success depends upon the level of subject matter expertise that you can tap into. It is important to know when you are in over your head. It is also important to know when you can accelerate your progress through expert mentoring. When it comes to hiring a coach, you need to be ready for a long-term relationship based upon the coach's expertise and your comfort with how that coach communicates. With so many specialists to choose from, it is important that you have a strategy for selecting your ideal coach/advisor—a screening process. For example, you need to know:

★ Background—Who is your prospective advisor?

★ Unique Value and Expertise—What does the coach do?

★ Beliefs and Motivation—Why does the coach do it?

★ Process and Professionalism—How does the coach do it?

★ Clientele—Who has the coach done it for?

★ Differentiation and Uniqueness—What makes this coach different?

★ The Real Value—Why should you do business with this coach?

These seven questions, which comprise the Pusateri Value Ladder™ developed by management consultant and value expert Leo Pusateri,[6] provide a structure to formalize the selection and screening process. With these points covered, you will be in a much better position to understand what the coach's expertise is, how the coach can help you, and whether you are comfortable with the risks associated with his or her type of business process.

Your Coach/Advisor Screens You, Too

You can see that your selection of a screening process can play a big role in ensuring you get as close to your ideal advisor relationship as possible. Defining your ideals plays a big role in successfully establishing your goal and identifying those who help achieve your goal. It is important to remember that while you are screening your potential advisor for skills and aptitude, this person is screening you, too—or should be!

What about the other side of the coin? What do you and your goals represent to your prospective advisor? Are you a warm body with a wallet? Are you an interesting challenge to be solved? Are you more than just an opportunity to apply theory? Are you providing your potential advisor with an opportunity to work within his or her area of specialization and an opportunity to perfect skills—either now or in the future? While you are seeking an advisor to help with your goal achievement, congruency also implies that your advisor is working towards his/her personal

[6] Pusateri Value Ladder™ reprinted with permission from Leo Pusateri and Pusateri Consulting and Training (www.pusatericonsulting.com).

goals, too.

Remember, you are seeking congruency. You should be your ideal advisor's ideal client. Your advisor must be able to address your needs. And, to create the ideal relationship, you need to fit into the practice your prospective advisor is building.

Having a coach/advisor provides you with structure, resources, knowledge, and perspective to save you time. That way, you will produce superior results sooner. Ideally, your prospective coach/advisor will have the understanding of your goal to construct a "success checklist" for you. With this valuable tool, you will have a map that takes into consideration your values and goals, your commitment, your time horizon, your resourcefulness, and the nature of the relationship you want to establish.

Meeting With Your Coach/Advisor

The more often you meet with your coach, the more feedback you will receive. However, there comes a point of diminishing returns where the value received does not exceed the price being paid. How often you meet depends on factors such as:

★ What you are trying to accomplish

★ What level of accountability you need

★ How much time it takes to show results

Once the basics are in place, many people only need to meet about every 90 days. Any less often and you might find that your commitment and accountability decline. Meeting more frequently might become unnecessarily expensive and can shift the relationship from one of benefiting from the coach's expertise (proactive) to creating a dependency (passive). Having a quarterly review highlights one of the Living On Purpose Paradigm's key elements—The 90-Day Follow-Up Strategy.

What To Pay Your Coach/Advisor

When the student is ready, the teacher will appear.

—Indian Proverb

The topic of compensation always reminds me of Goldilocks and the three bears. We are always afraid that we will pay too much, and we are happy to get extra value for less. We are rarely concerned that we will pay too little. The question is, "How do you determine whether the consultant's fee is just right?" Just as with Goldilocks, sometimes it will be and sometimes it will not. Your investment in support and advice should depend on your ability to benefit from the information you receive. A novice goal setter might consider a $20 book or a $100 subscription to a motivation website to be expensive. An experienced goal setter might consider the goal achievement benefits of a year's one-on-one coaching far outweigh the $5000 contract price. It is all a matter of preparedness, perception, need and choice.

So many choices to make. Choosing your strategic position. Choosing your asset and goal to work on. Choosing your Tactical Goal Achievement Process. Choosing whether to seek out a coach/mentor. Choosing the best coach/mentor. But are these choices all important? You bet they are! Your choices influence your outcomes. Just about all of humankind's progress has been as the result of choices made to get out of a rut and do something differently. Mass emigration from 19th-century Europe colonized much of North America while at the same time easing the pressure on the food supplies in Europe. Once across the Mississippi River, pioneers of the mid-1800s saw this sign at the start of the Oregon Trail that led into the American West: "Choose your rut wisely; you'll be in it for the next 2,000 miles!"

Your choices, including the financial ones, determine whether you stay in a rut or move over to the path to success. *Make sure all of your choices line up with your goal statement.*

Chapter 14
Choosing Good Habits =
Creating Best Practices

The ability to freely choose is considered one of our fundamental freedoms. Human history recounts the heroic efforts of people turning their worlds upside down to be free to choose their thoughts, their friends, their opportunities, their words, their religious or philosophical beliefs. Many of the choices we make open doors to new opportunities or to the commitment to our convictions. In moments of quietude, people sometimes think about what might have happened had they made different choices—moved somewhere, married someone else, taken a different job—the list is endless.

The focus of the Living on Purpose Paradigm is to create a future based upon purposely chosen actions, regardless of how old you might be. Choice implies alternatives to chose among. Once a goal topic has been decided upon, a virtual cornucopia awaits the goal setter. Some choices are logical, others are intuitive; many (such as why eating five small meals can help you lose weight) appear to be neither. Action based upon consistent and informed decision making leads to goal achievement success.

Every goal implies a Goal Achievement Process. Every process requires that specific actions are identified and used to create the momentum needed to achieve your goal. Major goals require major momentum, which comes from understanding what you need to do, when, and why. This is fundamental to your successful progress.

Whether you decide to hire a coach or strive to achieve your goal success on your own, you will most likely be working on a lifestyle habit you either want to create or eliminate.

Goals usually involve (a) giving up something, (b) doing more of something, (c) doing something different, or (d) doing something less frequently. The "something" is quite often a habit (or behavior or way of thinking—basically, these are all the same) you have acquired over years of dedicated practice. You can see that it is holding you back. You can see the potential just out of reach. You can outgrow any habit and shake it off. As a goal achiever, your future will offer new capabilities and open new doorways to opportunities formerly out of your reach. Think of yourself as a caterpillar evolving and developing new capabilities to become a butterfly, able to soar to new personal heights!

Take a moment and list some of the habits you have, want to develop or want to get rid of, or are perfecting, in Exercise 24.

Exercise 24: Habits To Cultivate, Eliminate… Or Keep

Whole Person Concept Category	Good Habits I Want to Develop and Perfect	Bad Habits I Want To Eliminate	Bad Habits I'm Going To Keep —Anyway!
1. Physical			
2. Spiritual			
3. Social			
4. Intellectual			
5. Financial			

Habits are things that you do without thinking. They fall into many categories—for instance, personal hygiene, travel routes, how you dress yourself, and so on. Habits make life easier by establishing personal standards of acceptability. Executive consultants speak about companies having "best practices." Your habits are your personal "best practices." They determine how you get things done.

Sometimes one's personal best practices are the same as other people's; sometimes they are uniquely yours. What if your best practices are producing *negative consequences* rather than *positive results?* Best practices should not be confused with favorite habits. Your reading habits or vocabulary can open or close the doors to interesting career and social opportunities.

How do you identify and change your uniquely less-than-perfect habits?

Well, the "identify" part is easy—you probably know lots of people who would be happy to identify them for you. The more important question is, "How do you break a habit?" Simply stated, you just replace it with a different habit—which is easier said than done. Habits come with comfort, safety, and emotional dimensions. Many habits reduce stress and provide security, making them particularly difficult to change.

In their extreme, addictive habits such as alcoholism can be compulsive and self-destructive. Behavior modification sciences have developed techniques, templates, and processes around the rehabilitation of individuals with the most destructive types of habits. One of these processes is often called a "12-Step Process." The most familiar of the 12-step processes is that defined by Alcoholics Anonymous. Other 12-step groups have modified the steps slightly to create a more generic approach as laid out below.

The 12-Step Process[7]

1. We admit we are *powerless* over our addiction—that our lives have become unmanageable.

2. We *believe* that a Power greater than ourselves can restore us to sanity.

3. We make a *decision* to turn our will and our lives over to the care of God as we understand God.

4. We make a searching and fearless *moral inventory* of ourselves.

5. *We admit* to God, to ourselves and to another human being the exact nature of our wrongs.

6. We are *entirely ready* to have God remove all these defects of character.

7. We *humbly ask God* to remove our shortcomings.

8. We *list* all of the persons we have harmed, and we are willing to make amends to them all.

9. We make direct *amends* to such people wherever possible, except when to do so would injure them or others.

10. We continue to take *personal inventory* and when we are wrong promptly admit it.

11. We seek through prayer and meditation to improve our *conscious contact with God* as we understand God, praying only for knowledge of God's will for us and the power to carry that out.

12. Having had a spiritual awakening as the result of these steps, we try to *carry this message* to other addicts, and to practice these principles in all our affairs.

[7] Kindly provided by V.B. of Deep Health Network.

Severely well-entrenched habits can require Herculean effort to "simply" replace them. It you can successfully give yourself a "kick" with much less effort, count yourself lucky and just do it. Life is too precious to willingly surrender your self-control. It is up to you to say "Enough!" and take action in the areas that need it most.

Behavior Modification

Often people turn to psychologists who specialize in behavior modification techniques. The psychological discipline of behavior modification is a field of clinical psychology that relies on rewarding positive behavior to increase its frequency over less desirable, unrewarded behavior. Here is an example:

Step 1: Evaluate and admit to your current status with the behavior (habit) that you want to change.

Step 2: Identify the desired behavior.

Step 3: Choose a reward for success.

Step 4: Choose a consequence for failure.

Step 5: Be consistent.

Step 6: Monitor, record, and reward progress. (Do not reward failure.)

Step 7: Add variety and repeat.

(You may notice strong similarities between Steps 2–7 and our Six-Step Tactical Goal Achievement Process. This is not accidental! Our goal setting process does employ the same scientific discipline and methodology.)

Once you focus on the habit or lifestyle change that you want, it is time to take action. Part of your habit-changing program involves knowing what you want, why, and when. You want to remove temptation by changing your environment and your routines, or by creating different connections and associations between things. Sometimes it is best to take baby steps, like reducing the amount of sugar and cream in your coffee.

Lou's Law Of Propinquity

Propinquity—is that really a word? Yes it is. More about *propinquity* in a minute!

Even if you love coffee but want to lose weight, consider the following:

At first blush, the thought of replacing your coffee habit with a water habit would seem to take a lot of effort for little benefit. However, this could have a very significant impact.

Many years ago, I averaged between 15 and 20 cups of coffee a day. Ya! I agree—way too much caffeine! (Chocolate? Cola? Let's not even go there.) Thankfully, I was able to break my habit. But how much do you drink? If you grab a large coffee on your way to work followed by a coffee break in the morning, coffee at lunch, and a coffee break in the afternoon, you are drinking at least 4 to 6 regular-sized cups a day. If you take your coffee "double double" each day, you are consuming at least 8 teaspoons of sugar and a lot of cream. (Oh my goodness—48 teaspoons equals one cup of sugar!! That's a cup of sugar every six days—over two pounds of sugar a month!) And what would a coffee be without a cigarette or a donut? Or both!!

What if you switched from coffee to water—from "double double" to an apple or orange? Who would want a cigarette (or a donut!) with an orange? Good habits replace bad, your diet improves, calories are reduced, sleep improves, life expectancy increases, and you have a few extra dollars left over too. This is a good trade-off that moves you towards your health goal. You could even tie this into a financial savings goal. Obviously you need to do more, but it is a great start at changing your habits.

Now for *propinquity*. One of the best ways to stop eating cookies, French fries, or cheeseburgers with bacon is to stop buying them. I am sure it could be scientifically proven that people do not eat foods they do not have access to. It is common sense, really. If you do not have cookies to eat, you will not eat cookies. You will substitute something else for the cookie— perhaps an apple or some carrot sticks. So you can see how your choice of behaviors allows you to shape your destiny around achieving your goal. By living on purpose, you shape the future that you want to create. Is this a Herculean effort? No. Would it be a major step towards weight loss and a healthier heart? Yes!

I call this Lou's Law of Propinquity. (*Propinquity* refers to physical proximity, or closeness.) This law states that you will eat (or do) whatever is closer (or easier) before you will opt for a more difficult, less convenient choice. Rocket science? Nope! Just common sense.

Proactive change will produce positive results. You may choose to take more direct action like not buying chocolate chip cookies or taking the stairs instead of the elevator. From a career perspective, habits such as punctuality or good grooming can produce major results. Building your leadership capabilities through joining Toastmasters will enhance your self-esteem and give you a skill that will open doors and create opportunities that you will cherish forever.

Think positively. Remember what you want and why. Reinforce your positive behavior. Reinforce your self-image and perception of yourself as someone with different habits. Create alternatives for yourself that lead in your desired direction. These actions are intended to connect you with what you want and attract more of it into your life. (That sounds remarkably like the law of attraction—but with a constructive proactive twist. After all, goal achievers know that there is no free lunch.)

Tying Your Habits To Your Goals

So how do your habits tie into your financial, physical, social, spiritual, and intellectual goals? Consider the following (they are all examples of habits): Attitudes about money and spending habits can make or break your financial health. *When* and *how much* you eat can be just as important as your food choices to your physical well-being. How you relate to your family and co-workers, your communication methods, and attitudes towards specific people and social situations affect how others react and respond to you. Your energy conservation efforts, together with everyone else's, will impact the quality of future life on our planet. Your perception, your understanding, and methods of coping with the aspects of life that lie outside your control affect your spiritual health, how you react to stress, and how you think about the future. Your reading habits affect your knowledge as well as your ability to assimilate information and make sense of the events in your life. Living within your means results in extra money for investing. Distinguishing strategic investing as different from recreational gambling or lottery speculation will perpetuate your wealth.

Through strength of character and personal resolve, you may be able to suddenly dislodge a habit. However, because habits develop over time, they rarely totally disappear overnight. They are created by repetition and reinforcement, and can only be weakened by choosing, repeating, and reinforcing an alternate behavior. Another way to look at this is to say that habits are the actions you practice doing. The more you practice something, the better you get at it. When you want to weaken or stop a habit, you need to stop practicing it—and you can do this overnight...after night...after night. Consistently create your new habit. Since you found comfort in the old habit, you may find yourself coming back to it in spite of your best intentions. Remember, this will also require breaking the emotional, security, and comfort bonds associated with the behavior and shifting these attributes to the new behavior that you want to develop.

Habits are attributes of your "self." Understanding your habits and their effect on situations you want to change will move you closer to achieving your goals. After all, you do want your habits to become your personal best practices!

PART FIVE

Pulling It All Together

SYNERGY

When the whole is greater than the sum of its parts

SERENDIPITY

Not only finding things by good fortune, but also realizing that you have found something. Many apples fell from trees before Isaac Newton was inspired to "discover" gravity.

Chapter 15
Combining The Categories Of
The Whole Person Concept

So far, you have focused on each of the five Whole Person Concept categories separately, but I am sure you understand that they do not function in isolation. Your Whole Person Concept's assets are constantly interacting with each other, placing greater or lesser emphasis on any one area at any one time. Your assets work in harmony and a synergy develops between your asset categories—and in turn, between your goals. These ultimately result in the "old you" morphing into the "new you."

So who are you? Who do you want to become? You will find your answer when you look to your goals. When your assets work in union, they form dyads (2s), triads (3s), tetrads (4s), and pentads (5s). Combine any two assets and you create a synergy where the whole is truly greater than the sum of its parts.

Just as a dog sled can be pulled by one dog struggling bravely, or by several dogs working in powerful union, the momentum of your major goals working in tandem will create ever greater power and efficiency. When your assets work in union, they will drive and channel your energy in new directions created by and yet creating your greater purpose, fitness, leadership, and other capabilities on both a personal and a public level.

Consider the following dyads and where they might lead:

Intellectual Health + Spiritual Health = Personal Leadership: When you combine the strengths of Intellectual Health with Spiritual Health, you have a power combination of factors necessary for Personal Leadership to make you a capable role model and an inspiration to others.

Intellectual Health + Social Health = Personal Purpose: Combining Intellectual Health with Social Health helps you develop your Personal Purpose in life and work towards your goals in a more directed manner.

Financial Health + Physical Health = Personal Fitness: Physical Health and Financial Health give you the funding necessary to achieve your own best Personal Fitness. Adding your Spiritual Health drives your desires for contribution and for a strong body, creating a synergy and vision that could spur anything from a breakfast program in inner city schools to programs intended for defeat of AIDS in Africa.

Financial Health + Social Health = Public Leadership: When you harness the strength of your Social Health with Financial Health, you can fund an active public leadership role in politics or support special ecological interests.

Physical Health + Spiritual Health = Personal Capability: Combining your Physical Health Asset's goals with your Spiritual Health Asset's goals produces personal capabilities that give you the strength and energy to follow your dreams and live your convictions.

Financial Health + Spiritual Health = Personal Philanthropy: The role of your Financial Health's assets as a funding source for all the others cannot be underestimated any more than the importance of the Spiritual, Physical, Social, or Intellectual Health components. They are all significant in their own right and in combination with each other.

The Whole Person Concept defines five key areas. Earlier we noted that, symbolically, you could take any one of your Goals Incubators and link it to the corresponding Goal Achievement Process within the never-ending belt created by the Major Goals Momentum Systems and The 90-Day Follow-Up Strategies. Doing this creates a powerful goal achievement dynamo. When all five dynamos function in unison, you create a pentad. This is depicted in Diagram 9, The Pentad. It depicts the figure eight relationships created for all five Whole Person Concept categories interrelating and working together. The intent of the Living On Purpose Paradigm is to help you create your own personal pentad firing on all cylinders—that is when your life is in balance, all five Whole Person Assets are humming at capacity, and your life is one of contented accomplishment.

Diagram 9: The Pentad

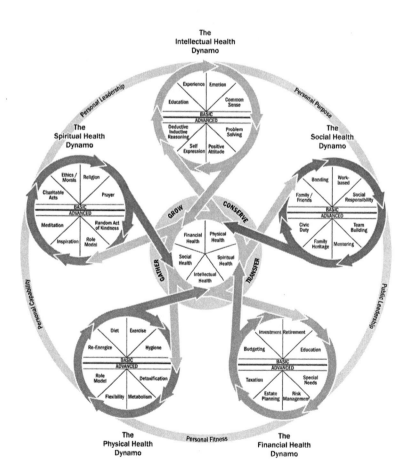

The Pentad, Copyright © 2009 Lou Mulligan. All Right Reserved.

To me, creating your own personal Living on Purpose Paradigm Pentad is the ultimate goal: having strong goals in each of Physical, Spiritual, Social, Intellectual and Financial Health areas that work together to create a better person and a better world. As you work to improve your Living on Purpose Paradigm system, you elevate your goals. Your need for a higher level of sophistication and support may create a need for coaches/advisors who can provide a higher level of value-added support. Do not worry when this happens; it is important to keep your goals congruent with your needs and obtain adequate support to carry you to your next level.

Hey! I Can Do This is not a "one-time read." It is a book that will have greater meaning for you as you progress in your goal achievement efforts. As you advance in each of your goals, take time to revisit and update your data based on your new status. Use your Goal-Setting Blueprint sheets for each of your goals to rework and reset the bar as you advance your Whole Person Concept Tactical Goal Achievement Process models for your best next level. By doing this, you will give your "you" a new understanding and an unstoppable sense of progress and satisfaction!

Chapter 16
Barriers, Boxes, And Self-Limitations

Remember our discussion about self-talk in Chapter 8? Sometimes, you might get bold enough to engage in self-talk out loud and even share it with other people. Imagine the power of vocalizing your self-talk and getting someone else to agree with you! Talk about vindication! If someone has already agreed with you, how could you ever change? Why would you even need to *consider* changing?

At one time or another, everyone has defined himself or herself as a "failure" in something. Here are a few examples you have either heard of or can identify with:

★ "I'll never learn to walk," thought the 10-month-old baby after falling down the 249th time.

★ "I'm no good at giving speeches," said the future politician after forgetting his memorized speech in seventh grade.

★ "I'll never become a musician," said the future rock star after "freezing" at a piano recital when she was 10 years old.

★ "I'll never learn how to ride a bicycle. It's just too difficult to keep my balance!" said the future cycling champion.

★ "I'll never be able to shoot hoops," said a soon-to-be NBA All Star player after getting cut from his high school basketball team for being too short.

Moments of self-declared failure are not the end of the world. They are opportunities to face your momentary "impossible" goal and build character by moving ahead and make "doing it" your commonplace experience. The good news is that all these "nevers" were overcome (or can be overcome) by just about anyone. With patience and effort, humor, and confidence building, the impossible becomes possible.

**If you change the syntax a little,
"impossible" becomes "I'm possible!"**

Hiding In A Box

There were times when you might have chosen to place yourself neatly into a "box" by raising barriers to keep others out or restrict your development in a skill area. Hiding inside a box was comforting because you no longer needed to stretch beyond its limitations or think beyond your experience. You no longer needed to challenge yourself. But boxes are limiting. Once in a box, what once was your "challenge" gradually evolves towards becoming impossible. Take for example, the second-grade female subtraction superstar who heard that math was nerdy and boys don't like nerdy girls. Thus, the "I'm no good at math" gal was born, and she gradually turned into an "I can't do math" woman. The need to be popular converts enjoying the structure of mathematical challenge into an impermeable numbers barrier. Balancing a checkbook becomes an impossible obstacle. Income tax preparation creates overwhelming anxiety. But that same gal could be a computer gaming whiz and still be popular because "gaming" is cool! (Not to mention that it takes an analytical capability that probably rivals the greatest minds of 14th-century Europe.)

No matter who you are, *you are not the permanent resident of any box. You are only a guest. You are free to move on!* Through goal-focused patience and directed effort, you can escape from practically any box you have chosen to climb into.

How You Define Yourself

Self-definition allows you to eliminate wide ranges of potential present and future options. For example, if you are a "people person" and not comfortable in solitary pursuits, you will probably never have to worry about writing a book. Regardless of how badly you might want to, book writing has solitary aspects. If you cannot dictate it or turn it into a party, it likely will not happen.

Keeping others "out" and yourself "in" reduces your options, too. The limitations of self-definition create a comfort zone that you might never have to leave. But is this in your own best interest? Will it make you a better person? Will it enhance your contribution to the world or your ability to help your children find answers in their lives?

Public speaking is one of the greatest fears of most people. A root canal seems less threatening than standing in front of an audience and publicly speaking your mind. When you define yourself as afraid to speak in public, you define yourself away from pleasurable and career-advancing opportunities to mingle with others and demonstrate that you have the skills and ability to lead. It is amazing how a small action like taking a six-week community college course in public speaking, joining an acting group, or spending a year in Toastmasters can turn a career-limiting self-definition into a stepping-stone for lifelong advancement.

Self-definition has a positive side. Once realized, it can be your ticket out of the box. Listen to your self-talk. Pick an area of debilitating limitation that holds you back and say,

> **"I'm not the kind of person who lets _____ limit my enjoyment and progress."**

Say it again…

> **"I'm not the kind of person who lets _____ limit my enjoyment and progress."**

Now, believe it.

Do something about it. It is not skydiving, it is not brain surgery. (However, at a certain level, I guess it might be!)

Take positive action! Now!

The Math Quiz Paradigm

For many people, adding, subtracting, multiplying, and dividing become a mystical challenge. Others feel the same about road maps…How long?…How far?…Which turn? Time and distance are fascinating subjects. There is the speed at which time passed when you were totally bored as a child and the time that flies by when you are an adult on vacation. There is thirty minutes in a dentist's waiting room and thirty minutes with your sweetheart. It is hard to believe they are the same. The "Are we there yet?" distance that children experience in a car makes desperate parents find inventive ways to distract them (such as counting brown Toyotas or looking for Virginia license plates). The "Where has the time gone?" adult, with so much on her mind, might relish the change to have time drag by again. (Personally, we used to ask our children simple mathematical equations like "What is 27 + 46?" Boy, did that keep the back seat quiet! Our kids did learn their mathematics.)

Then there is scientific distance—precise and measurable. There was a time when most people did not know the exact length of a mile or how long a minute lasted. Sure, there was the distance from here to that tree and back, but that varied depending on the tree's location. Under that mind-set, any race had to be "head to head"—never against the clock or an ideal. With the advent of standardized measurements, the precision of the 5,280-foot mile and the 60-second minute were invented and everyone agreed upon what they meant. A new "scientific" box was created for every aspiring Olympic-level middle-distance runners. Scientific boxes are based upon "facts," so they are particularly sticky! The physical impossibility of the sub-four-minute mile was one of these facts. The following *math* quiz outlines the dilemma. (It's easy! Honest! I've even provided the answers!)

Question	Answer
What is 86,400?	The number of seconds in a day (easy—that was at the start of Chapter 2.)
What is 3,600?	The number of seconds in an hour.
What is 240?	The number of seconds in four minutes.
What is 5,280?	The number of feet in a mile (that should be an easy one).
What is 22?	The number of feet that you need to cover each second to run a mile in four minutes.

What's the dilemma? How could anyone ever run that fast (22 feet per second) for that long (4 minutes)?!

Roger Bannister's Breakthrough

From the time we could precisely measure the 60-second minute until Roger Bannister's historic foot race, scientists deemed that for a man to run a mile in under four minutes was a physiological impossibility. *Everyone* knew that the human body could not withstand the stress and strain that running a mile in less than four minutes would require. *Everybody knew. It was a scientific fact! Your lungs and your heart would explode!* Yet on May 6, 1954, Bannister's time was 3 minutes, 59.4 seconds—the fastest mile ever run to that date. An impossible accomplishment! Yet since then, Bannister's record time has been lowered on 18 different occasions. By August 2001, sub-four-minute mile runs had been officially recorded over 855 times.[8]

[8] http://web.telia.com/~u19603668/atb-m07.htm.

Today, the ability to run a sub-four-minute mile is considered the basic qualification for an elite, middle-distance runner. The current record, which was set in Rome in 1999 by Hicham El Guerrouj of Morocco, is 3 minutes, 43.13 seconds.

Once one person steps beyond a paradigm's limitations, many others follow!

Interestingly, Bannister's record time was first bettered only 46 days later by Australian John Landy. Like Bannister, once you show the way, others' superior record-breaking performance is sure to follow.

The barrier had been broken.

Presumption was no longer the same as fact.

The paradigm has shifted.

In this example, the four-minute mile was a "box." Boxes are paradigms—prisons that you are meant to escape, limits meant to be surpassed. You each have one. What is your totally impossible four-minute mile? Make it "I'm possible!"

As you know, goal setting and goal achievement imply risk to your ego. When you set a goal and work towards achieving it, you are stepping outside your comfort zone. When you step beyond your former limitations, you are creating a "new you" with ever-increasing capabilities and capacities.

It is almost always worth doing.

In my financial planning practice, I have had numerous examples of individuals who have set targets of achieving financial independence, buying a home, financing their children's education, starting a business, or retiring early. All have benefited from the strategies outlined in this book; many have moved to a higher station in their lives.

Chapter 17
Multitasking And Other
Forms Of Self-Sabotage

How many things can you focus your attention on at one time? One? Two? Three? Five? Eight? (Ah ha! A Fibonacci sequence! The next number is thirteen. But I digress.) Being impressed by how smart you think you are (like I just did) is a form of self-sabotage, so I'd better get back on track. Actually, this provides a chance for a little humility. I first learned about the Fibonacci sequence from one of my sons when he was in fifth grade. (So, I may be a university graduate, but I'm not smarter than a fifth grader!)

Can You Relate To This Scenario?

We live in a frenzied age. The time of Y2K (Remember Y2K—the time-machine-like non-event where all computers were supposed to think it was 1900 instead of 2000?) heralded more than a new century and new millennium. It also heralded a new way of thinking, working, learning, communicating, organizing, and...wasting time. Let's see, as I write this, I am watching television, audio muted, closed-captioning on while listening to the FM radio. Simultaneously, on my computer I have two or three messaging groups open, my e-mail is online, and my calendar is open—just in case. Of course, my PDA and cell phone are also switched on (vibrate option). After all, I need to stay in touch!

So, where is my attention? What is my priority right now?

What am I focused on?

Many of my clients routinely receive over 100 new work-related e-mails every day and are expected to handle them on top of their other priorities. Many companies have instituted the policy that e-mails will be replied to within 24 hours. Having said this, I have yet to address anything that remotely resembles a priority—this is all just background noise.

My real priorities must compete with my multitasking. Do they have a chance? I hope so. After all, I KNOW what my priorities are. But what about the tenth-grade student? University student? Young parent? Each of them tries to cope with peer pressure, deadlines, insomnia, money issues, relationship demands and difficulties, overbearing parents or employers, absent parents, aged parents, drugs, sex, acceptance, rejection, and noise, noise, **NOISE**. Lots of luck!

In high school when I did cross-country running, my coach told me, "Never look at your feet. If you do, you'll stumble. Always look as far ahead as you can."

When I learned how to drive a car, my driving instructor said, "Never look at the oncoming traffic. If you do, you'll steer into it. Look as far down the road as you can, and drive towards that point." Given this advice, when and how did I become short-sighted? What causes me to lose perspective, to become harried? How do I get centered? Regain control?

Multitasking is becoming an epidemic. It is an institutionalized form of self-sabotage! It scatters your focus, your effort, and your priority. It sidetracks your progress-oriented activities. To be successful, you need "to look as far ahead as you can," to focus your concentration on one priority at a time and do that one thing until it is finished. This is the message of our Priority Reset Button in Chapter 11.

Self-sabotage is doing other than what you should be doing. Self-sabotage takes many forms. The end result is that you turn your back on successful goal achievement progress and return to your former station. An example is plugging in to peer group pressure to the extent that you cannot progress beyond the group. It is said that when cooking lobsters, there is no need to put a lid on the pot because the lobsters will always pull each other back into the boiling water—a harsh but vivid example of the sabotage of peer pressure.

Fear Of Success

Fear of success is an intentional form of self-sabotage. It happens when you find yourself outside your comfort zone in unfamiliar territory. Self-sabotage enables you to rope in your enthusiasm and bring yourself back to a former level of experience, capability, and accountability where your comfort is greater.

You might not recognize self-sabotage when it happens. You could just feel uncomfortable with your success or maybe you rest on your laurels. Either way, by allowing yourself to regress, you begin the descent back to your former self. Remember, *You don't have to go there.* By using the Major Goals Momentum System and The 90-Day Follow-Up Strategy you learned about in Chapter 12, you are free to keep your goals top of mind and maintain your forward momentum.

Stepping Beyond Comfort Zones

Ever hear of someone who won the lottery and went broke a year later? How about someone who got promoted over his capabilities and was on the street six months later? Why do these things happen? Having stepped beyond their comfort zones, they found themselves in the rarefied atmosphere of their Olympian gods—a mere mortal, unworthy to be in such august company—and so they took steps to ensure they would not stay there....

An unintentional form of self-sabotage is the natural tendency "to find the fences" or "test your limits." From early in life, you might have had a natural tendency to test the limits imposed on you, first by your parents and later by your peer group and work environment. You might have been one of the curious ones who saw a wet paint sign and could not leave it alone. You just had to know! Was it curiosity? Rebellion? Questioning if those boundaries really exist?

Needing to know your limits causes you to *find* them. Unsatisfied, you test your social relationships, or your Intellectual, Financial, Physical, and Spiritual Health—just to make sure things are as good as you think they are. To an age, most men think they are immortal. It goes with a man's innate ability (myself included) to find the shortest route to almost anywhere without a map. (Well, I did say almost!) "Heart attack, strokes, cancer—that will never happen to me. I'm in…great (gasp)…shape!" Testing the limits can mean acting out of character, or doing the opposite of what caused your success. These efforts can sabotage all of your good work. It is important to realize when you are engaging in self-sabotage and to get back on your path to success.

Passive forms of self-sabotage include the darker side of habits, rituals, and routines. Nonetheless, many habits and routines are good and productive. You may have developed these coping habits with little thought and turned them into personal activities. Useful processes like personal hygiene activities and driving the same route to work every day get you where you need to be, on time and in style.

Rituals are often associated with the religious aspects of spiritual health. They can be symbolic and comforting in their habitual consistency. As mentioned earlier, creating a habit takes approximately 21 days of consistent and faithful repetition to make it become part of your lifestyle. (Eliminating—or replacing—a habit might take longer.) Useful habits, routines, and rituals permit you to anticipate outcomes and achieve consistent results.

Like A Tug-Of-War Inside

Earlier, in the discussion of the "tipping point" concept in Chapter 8, I mentioned that there is a balance between what you have and what you want. When you set a new goal, you are doing it on purpose. You disturb this "tipping point" balance because you are trying to put more "weight" on the goal to be achieved. Many times, after successfully achieving their target, people slip back to their former ways and the scale returns to its former balance point. For the change to stick, your new success must bring a new balance point. You need to tilt the table such that the scale's balance point is consistent with your newly achieved goal. Backsliding towards your former balance point is "self-sabotage." The following excerpt from **www.Writing.com** provides an excellent explanation of self-sabotage.

> Self-sabotage is something we do to ourselves when we feel we don't deserve good things to happen to or for us. There is no logical explanation for why we don't or won't allow such things to happen. This is not for lack of desire for good things, rather, it's like a tug of war we play with ourselves inside between us wanting something good and not feeling worthy of it. Frequently using the word "should" is an excellent indication that one may be experiencing self-sabotaging behaviours.

> If there is no real reason for one to not experience good things, then self-sabotage is present.

> Self-sabotage can be a minor thing—a phase—or it can become so serious that it limits or completely destroys one's ability or desire to live the happy and fulfilling life we are all entitled to the moment we are born.

> Unfortunately, circumstances in life can severely alter our self-image to the point where we feel trapped in a never-ending cycle of unhappiness and lack of self-esteem and self-worth.

Here are some symptoms of self-sabotage—I've used the 15 most common symptoms that I see both in my own self and predominately in others, most of which are done subconsciously:

★ Procrastination

★ Destroying good or working relationships

★ Dissatisfaction with home life, career, relationships and life in general

★ Inability to control anger

★ Seeking out or staying in abusive relationships

★ Always putting one's self down, self doubt, belittlement of self ("I'm not worth their time" or "They shouldn't be doing this for me because I don't deserve it" or "I'm just in the way!")

★ Trust issues

★ Depression

★ Inability to finish what is started

★ Always having to have a "crisis" in life to feel purpose, or needing drama to feel fulfilled

★ Addictive behavior—broad spectrum

★ What do others think of me? Or how do others see me?

★ Weight loss with equal or more gain afterwards

★ Worrying excessively

★ Jeopardizing what is already good or working in life such as relationships, jobs, etc.

How to change:

First and foremost, one needs to be completely and sincerely honest with their self. To not be is also a form of self-sabotage because one can't address their issues if one continues to run and hide from what is holding them back!

How much are you're willing to do to work on yourself?

What are your goals?

Find out what you want, name your goals, make a plan to achieve those goals and then work hard to stick to those goals.

AFFIRM, AFFIRM, AFFIRM!!! Affirmations sound silly and corny but they're actually an excellent way to undo one's past way of believing they are not "worthy." How? Simply state the good things about yourself—daily and frequently.

All people are born worthy and good. Some people throughout their lives are told they are not good, they're not worth it, they're useless and etc. In time, they believe it.

Undo that damage. You believed those people—or yourself—when they told you those things, right? It's time to believe yourself when you are affirming the good things about yourself.

Each day, find five good things about yourself. Make a list, and make that list your personal bible. Carry it with you everywhere. State those affirmations. Add to the list constantly, without erasing the past affirmations.

In time, provided you were honest with yourself, you will begin to believe that Yes! you are a good and worthy person who is deserving of happiness and success!

Everyone has good—even people who are seemingly evil. How we choose to use our gifts is up to us.

And remember! Honesty to self is an all-important first step. Yes, the truth hurts. The truth really does set us free from what is holding us back, and what usually holds us back is ourselves.

Break free from the binds of your past.

And remember too as someone once said:

The best revenge is to live well [9]

Failure to overcome self-sabotage is just like loosening the chain of a bicycle, causing it to flap, buckle, and lose its fix to the sprockets. (This also alludes to the friction of The Pull of the Major Goals Momentum and The Push of The 90-Day Follow-Up Strategy. When this happens, the relationship between your strategic goals and values, and your tactical actions, breaks down. At first, it results in inefficiency and gradually deteriorates to a disconnect, squandering your energy and assets.)

Although it is destructive and counterproductive, self-sabotage in moderation can strengthen your commitment to the goal that you have successfully achieved. Through testing your theories, you prove the truth in them and add conviction to your actions. Just do not become enamored with the counterproductive behavior. Living on the edge might give a momentary thrill, but benefit from the results of your exploration and use it as part of your tactics to learn and grow.

[9] Wicked Ink has granted Writing.Com, its affiliates and syndicates non-exclusive rights to display this work. It can be found at http://www.writing.com/main/view_item/item_id/875665. © Copyright 2004 Wicked Ink (UN: lifewriter at Writing.Com). All rights reserved.

Take Ownership Of Your Future

Do test your theories if you must, but do so with the intention of better understanding your own Goals Incubator position and enhancing the asset-building goal processes that you are developing as you work through the exercises in this book. Take ownership! Embrace the magical interaction of "stimulus and response," of "cause and effect." Understand that you will create the future that you define for yourself. Use your daily trial-and-errors to gain experience and to gradually take ever increasing ownership of your future. Use your daily Priority Reset Button session to gain insight and forward progress to a bigger tomorrow.

This is also necessary so that you can take the steps towards perfecting the Living on Purpose Paradigm as it applies to your life (hopefully as the Pentad in Diagram 9 of Chapter 15). You can achieve this by focusing on your Major Goals Momentum System and by maintaining The 90-Day Follow-Up Strategy for each of your five Whole Person Concept categories. By using these two systems to power your goal achievement processes, you will grow in conviction and confidence in your efforts.

Chapter 18
So, Where Do You Go From Here?

It feels great to have created this definitive book on goal achievement. As the author, I am pleased that you have read this far and that you are committed to finishing the book. But adding another book to the field of self-improvement was never my objective. I hoped to share a better understanding of how to set and achieve goals that stick. *Hey! I Can Do This* is your practical guide to using goal achievement to create the life that you want and to attain those special enhancements that will give your life greater meaning and give you a greater sense of being truly alive.

For many people, just like quitting smoking, setting goals is easy...they have done it hundreds of times. They have lots of good intentions, but they lack the ability to persist in keeping their goal top of mind. The approach presented here, through The 90-Day Follow-Up Strategy and the Major Goals Momentum, is designed to create the momentum and personal accountability that are so often missing. With the Living on Purpose Paradigm's approach, you should be able to overcome years of goal setting frustration and to successfully apply the goal achieving techniques in all major aspects of your life.

This process integrates your values, assets, resources, goals, and objectives into a single framework. It gives you the ability to take your values and assets, and use them to develop workable, achievable, meaningful goals that fit you and your lifestyle.

Introducing the five components of the Whole Person Concept and interconnecting them with the Goals Incubator's four strategic stages aids in your awareness of the differing strategic expectations and their impact on the Six-Step Tactical Goals

Achievement Process.

The Major Goals Momentum System and The 90-Day Follow-Up Strategy provide both a pull and a push to keep you moving. The dynamic tension they create within your goals through adding the time-based momentum and accountability is necessary to keep the process moving towards your success. These dimensions provide structure and purpose to your good intentions. This momentum keeps you moving forward, achieving your major goals.

When you use the Major Goals Momentum System, you

1. Set your major goals in writing (focus)

2. Develop strategies and obtain resources for their attainment (empowerment)

3. Recognize their importance to you and keep working at them (persistence)

4. Utilize these three critical elements for goal achievement progress (momentum)

5. Create opportunities for synergy between the five dimensions of your Whole Person Concept

When you couple this with The 90-Day Follow-Up Strategy, you create goals that are more achievable because you

1. Add measurable and trackable targets

2. Add accountability of a progress evaluation

3. Add a definite time frame for progress evaluation

Taken together, you give your goals not only momentum, but also an extra push: the dynamic tension of a timetable and the accountability of a follow-up system. The Goal Setting Blueprints give your goals their 90-Day Milestones to achieve. However, even over 90 days, a goal can get away from you. Keeping it top of mind daily raises its visibility. Remember, there is also the added daily accountability of your Priority Reset Button, which gives daily detail to the milestones and stepping-stones of your personalized success checklist to bring you back on target.

A Quick Review

The Major Goals Momentum System is based on defining and making your most significant goals truly operational. Naturally, your goals will change in importance and immediacy over time. I recommend that you gradually work up to focusing on one goal from each of the five Whole Person Concept areas.

For each of the five Whole Person Concept assets, you answered this Mind-Stretcher Question: "If your success were guaranteed, what goals would you strive to achieve over the next three years?" Think about what will tip the scales in favor of the progressive change you desire. Focus on your goals, empower yourself, and establish persistence as you take the appropriate action—*every single day.*

Be open-minded and creative. Feel free to explore your goal areas from different perspectives. For example, your financial goal can include how you manage your cash flow, debt control, tax minimization, and other aspects of Financial Health. Your personal perspective gives meaning and life to every category.

To start, if you have not done so already, go back to Chapter 7 and finish the sections on goals and goal setting. Identify your five major goals. Remember to state each goal in a positive form. Evaluate each goal statement. Is it realistic, attainable, measurable...a worthy challenge? Revisit your goal statements in Chapter 10. Ask yourself, "Is it a goal with milestones that actually can be completed or is it a never-ending goal process?" Goal achievement requires a process; however, your goal statement should be a depiction of the "end" you want to accomplish. Rework your goal statement until you can give a positive answer to each of the following questions for each of your goals statements.

- ★ What will you have accomplished when you are done?
- ★ How will you know your goal statement is done?
- ★ How will you measure progress?
- ★ Can the goal be broken down into measurable stages?
- ★ What do you want to accomplish in each of the first five stepping-stones of the first milestone stage? What is the timetable for each step?
- ★ Where do you want to be at the end of the next 90 days?
- ★ How will you keep yourself on track?

There you have it. You have put the Major Goals Momentum System into effect. You have a written goal, The 90-Day Follow-Up Strategy, a sense of importance, and a sense of urgency. Now it is time to step up, see your target, and swing—put your plan into action!

Having a 90-day target makes the tracking process more interesting and more manageable. The 90-Day Follow-Up Strategy takes each of your goals and builds in accountability. The deadline creates the dynamic tension necessary to move forward with your goals towards the actualization of your values. To keep moving, you need to keep your five goals topmost in your mind. You need to review and take at least one small step forward on each goal every day. Do not let up. Keep moving.

You live a busy life and you have many priorities. Make an appointment with yourself, or if necessary, with a coach/advisor who specializes in The 90-Day Follow-Up Strategy. Stick to your commitment and review your progress. Set your program in place for the next 90 days. The 90-Day Follow-Up Strategy might sound basic, but it is the discipline and the structure of both the system and dedication of the few hours that you spend with it or your coach that keeps you focused on your goals and makes it all worthwhile.

Chapter 19
Reincarnation?

If you were to list your first assets, the ones you were born with, what would you include? For instance, would you answer be limited to your sex, your hair color, your ethnicity, your religion? Fortunately or unfortunately, you had no say in any of these. Yet, regardless of what these characteristics are and whether they have been helps or hindrances in creating your current self, you are still "you."

The question is not about which of these you chose and had control over. These comprise your birth resume. You have spent your entire life with them as your background. What you have done with these characteristics has determined how you took ownership of your life to create the person that you presently are. Now the question is, "How do you plan to take advantage of your current situation, current resources, and your current potential to create your optimum future?"

Your present is the result of your past efforts. It does not have to stop here. The question is: "What does your future hold?" Only you can set the goals that will take you there. Earlier we stated that your Living on Purpose Paradigm was:

When you purposely set goals and achieve them,

you can create a future that will be different from either your present or your past.

You can proactively pull yourself towards the future you want!

Creating your future in advance becomes your creative challenge. The "world" tells you what to do until you are somewhere between 16 and 25. After that, as an adult, you are pretty much on your own. Sure, you get clues from your career and peer group environments. You can always look backward at your accomplishments over time and intuitively know that you accomplished your past, but now we want to look to your future and create it in advance, regardless of your present.

You can create or re-create yourself. Through your hard work and effort, you have created the you that you see in the mirror. Can you describe the "who" you want to see in the mirror five years from now? Ten years from now?

It's 7/7/07. I'm watching "Live Earth, The Concerts for Climate in Crisis." It's amazing. For the first time ever, over 30% of the earth's population is simultaneously seeing and sharing the same information and messages. I have been watching broadcasts from Australia, Japan, China, Germany, England, South Africa, and the United States. I've listened to singers in German, Italian, Spanish, English, Portuguese, Chinese, and Japanese, to mention a few languages. Performances range from opera to 60's protest songs to contemporary rock. I did not understand it all, but I did understand the sentiment. From Sarah Brightman in Shanghai singing "Nessun Dorma" to Jane Goodall in New York, giving the welcome greeting shared between gorillas, the message was clear: "We need to unite.

SOS · · · − − − · · · The earth needs you."

Most needed no introduction. The latest performer —Josuf Islam—seemed vaguely familiar. I knew the voice, but not the name. After googling, I recognized him as Cat Stevens, a celebrity from 30 years ago. New name...but old music. Suddenly, he's completed his performance in Hamburg, Germany, and it's off to Madonna at Wembley Stadium in England. Josuf Islam is 59 years old and as charismatic, creative, and insightful as ever. Madonna is 50. Remember Madonna? She headlined the Live Aid show in 1985 and she's still a headliner. Her athleticism would put many younger women to shame. Both Madonna and Josuf have reinvented themselves. Age is not an issue. Passion and purpose are. Why shouldn't your purpose lead to a new you with the vigor to rekindle your youthful dreams and ambitions?

Your future is what you choose to make it.

You don't have to do things that you're not prepared to. You just need to do what's within your capabilities. For some, this means recycling paper, metal, and plastics; for others, it may mean much more. You decide whether and how you want to reinvest yourself...and then...you do it.

Racial and political boundaries are just details. Age and education are details too. Ultimately, it's just about you, what you want to accomplish while you're here, and what legacy you want to leave for your successors.

Marshall McLuhan, a Canadian university professor in the 60s said, "The medium is the message." I'm certain that he was right. It is estimated that today, over 2 billion people will hear the Live Earth message. How long before 4 billion— 66%—and eventually 99% of the earth's population have simultaneous access to and understanding of the same message at the same time!

Seeing Live Earth made me think about the impact of the baby boom generation. From prepackaged ready-to-serve baby food to fast food restaurants, from rock 'n roll to disco and beyond; from Volkswagens to Minivans and SUVs, this aging generation continues to leave its mark. Boomers have seen more technological innovation than any previous generation. Their children are seeing even more... and even faster change. The idealism, the energy, the ability to organize around principles and to question made the Boomer generation unique in the history of humanity. Currently, as boomers approach their retirement years, they are educated, affluent, visionary, and better able than any previous generation to influence the course of present and future generations. Many of these boomers' parents worked until they were too old and too tired, enjoying only a few short years of retirement prior to death. Now, as aging boomers, this current generation enjoys and expects more health care advances and the early retirement advantages that give them and their children the expectation of 30 to 50 years of productive leisure in retirement. Youthful idealism has been replaced by practical and pragmatic wisdom. Even now boomers still have 20 to 40 years of energetic leisure time to rekindle and channel their passions, their energies, and their interests, to study, to exercise, to relax, and to orchestrate change—to add value—to the world they will leave behind. This gives them as much time ahead as their entire past lifetime of career employment!

Just as Cat Stevens and Madonna have reinvented themselves, so can the rest of the baby boom and future generations. All you need is a reason and the ability to perceive and set new goals that allow you to channel your passion and energies towards creating a new sense of self—freer, more involved, more committed to your ideals. *Hey! I Can Do This* will be your key to this newer, bigger future—a future different from your past.

Can someone be too old for setting goals for their future? I believe the answer is "No." As long as you have someone, something, some ideal to live for, you have reasons to set goals and reasons to hope. Now that you have the knowledge of how to organize your goals into five categories according to the Whole Person Concept, you have a new way of looking at goal setting. As long as you can breathe, you can create a tomorrow that is bigger than yesterday. You can set and work towards your goals—physical, spiritual, social, intellectual, and financial.

Like a skilled potter at the wheel, you are shaping your future. What message do you want the future to hear? What role do you want to play? It's not too late. As long as you can set goals and work to achieve them, there's still time.

SOS ········· The earth needs you."

Chapter 20
What Makes You Feel Alive?

I started the first section of this book with the question: "What makes you truly feel alive?" We are back at the start, but with newfound wisdom. I hope you found reading and working through the exercises in *Hey! I Can Do This* to be thought-provoking, challenging, fun, and most of all, rewarding.

I want this book to be more than just a "feel-good self-improvement" book. I want you to get great value for the time you have taken to work through the theories and exercises, and I welcome your feedback about the effect that *Hey! I Can Do This* has on your life. Send me an email at **lou@HeyIcandoThis.com.**

Some people are natural goal setters; others are not. Only a true goal setter will read these pages. You are a goal setter. You know why you set goals. You know the benefits you have received. As Robert Browning wrote, "Ah, but a man's reach should exceed his grasp. Or what's a heaven for?"

Remember that in every action, every intention, there is a "stimulus" and a "response." The stimulus is what we do. The response is what we want! The responses can be many. Some can result from synergy, others from serendipity. You need to keep your mind open and focus on how you feel because of your initiatives. Your response is what you experience. The anticipated response is your motivation to do it. *Your anticipation of the response is what makes you feel alive*—so think about the things that make you feel alive. Ultimately, this is what you will want to do more and more of. Complete Exercise 25 to solidify the ideas in your mind. I have provided a start; feel free to add or delete as you see fit. I want this to become your list—a tool to help you better understand yourself and your goals.

Exercise 25: What Makes You Feel Alive?

Whole Person Concept Category	Some Possible Motivators	Some of Your Motivators	Actions You Will Take
Financial	Major purchases, house, car Entertainment/ technology System (toys) Business Investment		
Physical	*Taste* *Cheddar cheese* *Pumpkin pie* *Apple pie* *Touch* *Hot shower* *Making love* *Movement* *Dancing* *Feel of wind against my skin* *Flying a kite (feedback)* *Muscular exertion* *Sound* *Melodic music with a good Percussion, Syncopation* *Sight* *Smooth, flowing figures* *Beauty* *Vibrant colors* *Scenic vista*	Taste Touch Movement Sound Sight	

Spiritual	Meditation Church service Choral music Incense		
Social	*Being in love* *Being recognized*		
Intellectual	*Being in the groove of the moment (feedback)* *Paradigm shift-solving a mental challenge* *Public speaking*		

Think of what makes you feel dull and lethargic—lifeless. This *should* be what you would want to do *less* of. But when you get your wires crossed, you can confuse the two and develop habits of comfort or destructive risk taking (or risk aversion) that cause you to do those things that make you feel less alive, out of a sense of comfort and convenience. (These are those "bad habits.") Usually you can identify them as things that either over stimulate or deaden your sensory awareness.

Here is the good news. You know you have the tools to do something about it. Now you can take control of your life. You can create and take ownership of your future—on purpose.

Special Note To Readers

Having read *Hey! I Can Do This*, you may have questions or need more detailed examples for one of the five Whole Person Concept Assets. Special appendices to *Hey! I Can Do This* are located at **www.HeyIcandoThis.com.**

If you need additional copies of the exercises in this book, you can download them from the companion *Hey I Can Do This* website, creatively called **www.HeyIcandoThis.com.**

If you are interested in personal coaching in the Living On Purpose Paradigm, please contact us at **info@HeyIcandoThis.com.**

—Lou Mulligan

LaVergne, TN USA
15 April 2010
179287LV00001B/23/P